The Key to
Making Money
On Craigslist

The Key to
Making Money
On Craigslist

How I Make Thousands in My Spare Time

STEVEN FIES

The Key to Making Money on Craigslist

How I Make Thousands in My Spare Time

Edited by Marian Kelly
Published by Steven Fies
United States of America

Electronic Edition: December 2014
Library of Congress Control No.: 2014921476
ISBN 978-0-692-33546-8

For Whitney

Acknowledgments

I owe a great many thanks to the people who supported me in writing this book, which would not have happened if not for the suggestion of my friend and colleague Rob Acosta. Rob, I'm glad I stayed at work late that night and had that conversation with you about doing this!

Furthermore, I owe a great many thanks to my wife, Whitney, for supporting me through the journey of writing my first book, and to Gordon Kelsch, who so thoroughly helped me evaluate my first draft. I should also point out that Gordon also helped me with my first "flip" by fixing up a handle on an old speaker cabinet that became my first profitable sale.

I must also thank Rob Jones for getting me involved in this mess in the first place, and for being my partner in crime throughout the process.

Many more thanks must go to my friends and family, including Lora Fies, George Fies, Thomas Arthur, Gustavo Delgadillo, and the gentlemen from a band called Weight of the Sun, for supporting this process in countless ways and providing critical input where needed.

Last but certainly not least, the biggest thanks of all go to my editor, Marian Kelly, for crafting a halfway passable work product from my first scribbles. Her experience was invaluable in reworking many sections of this book, and without her developmental guidance I'm not sure this ever would have been published. She has a grasp of the English language that is second to none, along with a knack for making things flow. Thank you so very much, Marian, you are truly appreciated.

CONTENTS

FOREWORD

The first time I met Steven Fies was during my freshman year at the University of California, San Diego. We were assigned to the same dormitory suite, and it only took a few cordial greetings to know we were destined for a lifelong friendship full of memorable experiences together.

As I got to know Steve during college, what always stood out to me as special was his courage and determination to set bold, forward-thinking goals and accomplish them through great passion and extraordinary care. While many others struggled to keep up with basic course material, he would finish his class work and then push himself to acquire additional skills outside the classroom – business skills that would later prove valuable to the bottom line of life.

The most remarkable thing was how Steve made it seem effortless to dive into something completely new or out of his comfort zone and have great success. Fortunately for me, he didn't keep this ability a secret, and I was able to learn many lessons from him regarding how to approach life's challenges. Namely, how to take a smart risk, and how to achieve the positive frame of mind needed to push the boundaries with my own work.

All of this stuck with me after graduating from college, and eventually helped lead me to a decision that no one would have ever thought I'd make. Leaving the safe-haven of a comfortable career in biotech, I decided to pursue my dream of starting a tech company from scratch. Inspired in part by Steve's relentless will to always find a way, I knew my vision could become a reality once I harnessed my determination and took action.

Fast forward a few years and I have raised nearly $1M for my company. We launched in early 2013, and since then, I have had the opportunity to be featured on television and in famous news publications, meet some of the nation's top CEOs and business scholars, and recruit an incredible staff aligned with a unified mission to build software I never could have imagined before.

Importantly, all of this began when I conquered my fears and found the courage to take the first step.

What I like about The Key to Making Money on Craigslist is that Steve takes the time to show you exactly how to develop this courage, exploring the psychology behind it in enough depth that anyone can understand it. This is often the missing link between success and failure, as we tend to hold ourselves back more than anyone or anything else.

This book also walks you through the definitive steps you must take to analyze deals, negotiate effectively, and buy and sell at the right times – and at the right prices. The level of technical detail covered here is something this genre has never seen before, yet is explained so clearly that anyone can understand it. There is no doubt that you can make hundreds, if not thousands, of dollars when applying these principles.

However you choose to apply this knowledge, whether to Craigslist or a different resale market altogether, Steve has truly gone above and beyond in delivering an information product that is relevant, motivating, and immediately applicable to your life. This book will not only empower you to get motivated, get on your feet quickly, and succeed; it will provide you with business fundamentals that will serve you for the rest of your life.

Thomas Arthur
President and Co-founder of Lateral SV

INTRODUCTION

In seven months, I generated $3,827 on Craigslist by following the principles in this book.

This amount was the *profit* earned, not the gross sales volume, which was in excess of $10,000.

I generated another $2,126 in this same time period by selling existing inventory.

During the following several months (while writing the first draft of this book), I continued to buy and sell, ultimately ending the year with an additional$8,521 cash in my pocket. My total sales exceeded $20,000 for the year.

Since I have a full-time job, all of this happened during my free time, in just a few hours per week.

Now you might be wondering, "How can *I* go about generating hundreds, if not thousands, of dollars in my free time?"

It's simpler than you realize, but the majority of us choose to spend our leisure time relaxing on the couch, watching television, or surfing the internet. By getting a little more focused, you too can generate a few extra bucks.

By the way, when I started buying and reselling for a profit, I did not have a comprehensive book or guide like this one.

Sure, there were a few short blog posts and seventeen-page "books" available with quick tips, but they were unhelpful.

Why?

Well, we all love to focus on easy "tips" and tactics to help us achieve our goals, but they often fall short.

What diet pill will help me lose weight? Which pickup line will land me a date? How can I close a quick sale?

Quick tips that answer these questions make us feel good, but ask yourself honestly: How often do you actually use these tips? When you do, how often do they *actually* resolve your fundamental issue?

Probably not very often.

Yet we continue hoping that maybe one day we might stumble upon the magical quick tip or shortcut to certain success.

Realize: To truly be effective at something, we must invest the proper time learning the fundamentals, and then apply a proven system to achieve our goals.

This is why I have taken the time to develop a one-of-a-kind book for you. It features a proven system that can be learned and repeated, and no stone is left unturned. Every concept is explored in depth, and detailed examples are used to solidify key points.

Once you invest the time learning and applying these concepts, you will be armed with operating procedures that have already been tested, crafted, and fine-tuned through my own real-life experiences and successes.

Whether you desire to monetize a particular hobby, need to sell some of your current possessions, or just need some extra cash to pay bills, the recipe is right here for you.

What to Expect

In this book, you will:

- Learn how to analyze pricing, spot deals, craft killer advertisements, take intelligent risks, and negotiate successfully with others.

- Study real-life examples, actual transactions with buyers and sellers, and the underlying thought processes that lead to successful deals.

- Discover the hard and fast rules for instantly becoming more profitable and avoiding the most common pitfalls.

Beyond the book, I invite you to visit craigslist.stevenfies.com, where you can sign up for additional resources and information.

Please enjoy the read and may you have the best of luck in all your endeavors.

1

PREPARE FOR LAUNCH

A BIRD'S EYE VIEW OF MY SYSTEM

This chapter will give you a bird's eye view of what it looks like to buy and resell used items on Craigslist, including raising capital, acquiring inventory, and running through the sales cycle.

Preparation
Planning & Measuring
Deal Analysis
Purchasing
Sales

To start, we have a basic overview of the sales process. This is a simplified version of what any business may design as a flow chart for buying and reselling products or services.

In essence, you need some cash to get started, then you must invest that cash into items that you believe can be resold at a higher price, and finally you have to sell those items at a profit with reasonable consistency to create a sustainable system.

Principles of an Inventory-Based Business

1. Raise capital to go into business.
2. Purchase opening inventory.
3. Re-sell inventory at a profit.
   (An unspoken fourth pillar is "Rinse and Repeat.")

Let's discuss where these principles are covered in this book:

1. **Raising Capital:** In Chapter 3, we will discuss specific tactics for raising capital. There are more than a handful of viable methods presented there that anyone can tackle, even when starting from $0.00.

2. **Purchasing Inventory:** In Chapters 4-7, we will cover sound methods for finding and purchasing new inventory. Primarily, this includes how to scout for and identify good, profitable deals. There's some crossover into the sales component in these chapters, too.

3. **Reselling Inventory:** Finally, in Chapters 8-14, we will learn good sales, negotiation, and people skills to maximize profitability in resale.

You may have noticed Chapter 2 is missing from the above list. Chapter 2 is about getting into the right frame of mind for executing at a high level and being successful. It comes next because I want to get you psyched up and mentally prepared right at the outset. The importance of mental preparation truly cannot be overstated. We will squash any concerns or fears you may have in the next chapter.

Now, let's quickly review my recommended reading strategy for this book.

Reading Strategy for This Book

Generally speaking, I recommend reading through this book from start to finish, in the order the chapters have been laid out. There is a reason, after all, that the information has been provided in this particular order. However, there are some caveats to this:

Feeling Confident? If you are already feeling plenty confident in your abilities, feel free to skip over Chapter 2 and continue on at Chapter 3.

Already Have Money to Invest? If so, you can optionally skip Chapter 3, which is about raising funds. However, there are some good insights and stories there, so you may want to revisit it at a later time.

Short on Time? If you are short on time, or are eager to get into the real nuts and bolts of things:

Quickly skim through Chapters 4 & 5.
Read Chapter 6 in depth, followed by Chapters 10 & 11.
Visit the other chapters as needed.

Are You a Perfectionist? If so, read this book eighteen times, twirl in three circles, then recite it out loud (backwards).

Just kidding, of course. A note for perfectionists, though:

Chapters 4-14 form the key principles my system relies on to be consistently successful. However, there will always be an exception to every rule, so please do not feel obliged to follow these principles to the letter.

Obsessing over perfection might even cause you more harm than good, since you can wind up "getting in your head" too much and slow down your ability to act for fear of taking a misstep. Know that by following *most* of these principles *most* of the time, you will be fine.

More Detail on the "Big Picture"

Before we get too far ahead of ourselves, let's take a moment to review the big picture, including what to expect for the remainder of the book.

First of all, know that this is a sales gig. After all, my system revolves around buying and reselling merchandise on Craigslist. This means frequent emails, calls, and meetings with buyers and sellers, and necessitates a willingness to fail from time to time, too.

As a buyer, you will need to research available deals and make offers to sellers. You will probably need to make a lot of offers before you find sellers who are willing to take your offers, so do not be shy about emailing your offers out in bulk when the time comes. This is how you will acquire your inventory.

As a seller, you will need to post flashy listings that put your products in the best possible light, negotiate prices with buyers, follow up promptly, and push to set up appointments with incoming leads that express interest in your merchandise. This is how you will sell your inventory.

Eventually, once you are up and rolling, you will be performing both of these tasks simultaneously on an ongoing basis. You will be making offers, posting listings, meeting with folks, and completing deals.
Now, let's also address the law of averages.

The **law of averages** is a sales term that suggests a salesperson will close X% of his/her deals, where X is a fraction of Y total attempts to close. The implication is that more "attempts" yields greater sales volume.

While the law of averages is sometimes cited as a mathematical fallacy for reasons beyond the scope of this book, it is generally accepted in most sales and marketing assignments that more "attempts" will yield more closed deals.

The actual closing percentage, or conversion rate, can be improved with skill and experience, but the general principle still holds true.

As it does in most sales models, the law of averages will come into play for you, too. The more communication and contacts you have, the more buying and selling you will tend to do.

This is intuitive enough, but it often amounts to more work than some people realize, so we must learn to manage our expectations appropriately.

Specifically, we must know that, if we fall short on making enough contacts and keeping communication channels open, our results will suffer. This is "the rub."

On the other hand, if we commit ourselves to the process, maintaining a sufficient volume of contacts and communications, the sky's the limit.

Understand that committing to the process does not necessarily require a great deal of *time*, but there *is* a certain energy and focus required to convert leads and close deals.

This leads me to a strategic planning question:

Do you have a few hours each week to devote to a new project, and if so, when exactly are those times? Can you kick things into overdrive for those few hours to maximize your success?

The reason I ask this question is simple enough.

It is one thing to have a desire to succeed, but it is another to get out your schedule and pencil in the required actions to get there. No book, list of blog tips, or other A+ advice can help you without planning, execution, and follow-through.

Moving Forward

We all have an innate ability to succeed at much higher levels than we think. It may be necessary to do a little planning, learning, and moving past mental barriers, but the ability lies there within all of us.

This was something I did not fully appreciate myself until I was well into my own sales activities, and realized my average monthly *profit* was over $500. I never would have thought that to be possible in the beginning. But it happened, and I was able to continue proving my system worked in the following several months while writing this book.

Of course, mileage may vary, and I am not here to promise you an exact dollar amount that you will earn. Your achievement will largely be determined by the amount of your own effort and, to some extent, by the natural ebb and flow of the sales cycle. As in poker, you will be dealt different hands at different times and you cannot always expect pocket aces. But also as in poker, if you maintain a solid strategy over the course of many hands, you can do quite well.

Most importantly, what I know to be *absolutely true* is that, if you apply yourself, you can and will exceed your expectations, just like I did.

Whether you make $10, $100, $500, or even $1,000+ in a month, you can be successful and enjoy the challenge along the way.

CHAPTER 1 RECAP

- The three principles of an inventory-based business are raising capital, purchasing inventory, and selling.
- This is a sales gig involving ample market research and communication with buyers and sellers.
- The *law of averages* is a fancy way of telling us that "what we put in is what we get out." We still need good strategy, and eventually experience, to maximize our success; but this principle generally holds true.
- Success is only achievable through planning, execution, and follow-through. Make sure to identify what hours you can set aside each week for this project, and be prepared to focus during those times.
- Mileage may vary, but we all have what it takes to exceed our expectations and succeed at much higher levels than we realize.

Assignments

1. Identify the hours you have available to give to this project. Put some real thought into this, as your ability to commit is directly tied to your ability to succeed.

On Deck

In the next chapter, we will explore several "inner-game" mental and emotional strategies that are important to iron out before you go out there and start making deals. You need to sharpen your mind like a fine blade to stay disciplined, get organized, give yourself permission to take risks, and constantly push yourself to the next level.

2
SHARPEN YOUR MIND

FOUR WAYS TO ACHIEVE A WINNING FRAME OF MIND

This chapter is all about managing your internal world, including your thought processes and emotions.

Preparation
Planning & Measuring
Deal Analysis
Purchasing
Sales

In this chapter, you will learn why you must let go of your possessive nature, move past your fears with confidence, and adopt a positive attitude. I'll also provide specific methods to help you achieve these objectives. These are great life skills in general, and critical to success when starting what is essentially a small business.

The importance of mental preparation when undertaking a new task or challenge cannot be overlooked. With a proper "sharpening of the mind," people can do just about anything they set their hearts and minds to. Sports coaches, executive advisors, and personal counselors all know this, including it their programs and drilling it into the minds of their players and clients.

Entire books have been written on personal development, and while this single chapter does not go into that level of detail, it *will* explain several mental strength factors relevant to success in a small, inventory-based business.

If you are already a confident person, this chapter will simply nudge you into place before you move forward. On the other hand, if you struggle with self-confidence or motivation, it will challenge you to first address some core issues related to your thought processes – issues that might be real eye-openers for you.

Speaking of which, if you are interested in personal development at a deeper level, I would recommend picking up at least one self-improvement book and reading it alongside this one. Pick one from Amazon's current best sellers or from the list of suggestions I have posted in Appendix E.

Now let's dive into the meat of this chapter. Here is what we will cover:

1. Let Go of Your Possessive Nature
2. Face Your Fears
3. Learn a Useful NLP Trick

1. Let Go of Your Possessive Nature

The first step to sharpening your mind is to let go of your possessive nature with regards to material items, especially those that you intend to buy and resell. This means ceasing to look at items you buy as "things you own," and instead looking at them as inventory, or rather, business tools that are a simple means to an end – profit, of course.

Shifting your approach this way is very powerful. It removes any emotional attachment you might have had to a particular item and allows you to rationally make decisions about its purchase and resale. You need this rational decision-making power in order to succeed.

Oftentimes, when we buy new things (or used things), we get emotionally attached to them. There is a sense of possession that comes with purchasing and physically *having* something. You might not realize this, but it is true for the vast majority of people. This emotional attachment may stop you from selling your inventory if you are not careful.

Why do we get so attached? Well, consider the feeling you get inside when purchasing or inheriting something new and exciting. You now "own" it, and it has value to you. When you think about it going away or no longer being there, it triggers a sense of loss. You may experience all sorts of silly inner self-talk designed to help justify keeping the item in question.

"What if I don't ever find another one like this?"

"I got SUCH a great deal. Doesn't it make sense to keep this particular item... just this once?"

"This item is one of a kind! How could I ever let it go? Besides, it might be worth even more in a few years..."

What you are really saying in these examples is, *"It's Mine! You Can't Have It!"*

After all, we do have a primal instinct to protect our possessions. Realize, though, that this instinct is an obstacle on the road to success.

If you can cease to see items that you buy for resale as personal possessions, and instead start viewing them as *business inventory*, you will become more clear-headed and less emotionally attached.

When you achieve this frame of mind, your sales performance will increase, and in the long run you might actually be able to buy something to keep for yourself with all the money you've earned.

Let me repeat: *you must be clear-headed and remove any ideas about personal possession from your business operations.*

Here is an example of how this applies to me. I have been playing the guitar for fifteen years now. As a guitarist, I have a great appreciation for certain types of guitars and other instruments.

Every now and then, I purchase a guitar for resale that is really nice. My band members sometimes urge me to keep these items because they are "so awesome," or because I got such a "good deal."

Luckily, I know better. My side business cannot be profitable if I am always transferring my inventory *out* of the business and into my personal belongings.

Sometimes when I sell one of these rare and wonderful items, my band mates and friends will express disappointment, and even show a little pain at seeing such a great find disappear. As for me, though, I could not be happier, both inside and out. When great items disappear, it means I made a good sale, which in turn means I am doing well with my side business.

How to Let Go

If you struggle with letting go, consider participating in this exercise. This is optional, but may help you more quickly hone a strategic mindset that will benefit you in your dealings.

In this exercise, your task is to identify something currently in your possession that is valuable to you, and then sell it quickly, confidently, and without thinking twice. Even better if the item is something you cannot easily replace.

Please do not sell the most meaningful thing you have, though, because that certainly is not necessary for this exercise. Just understand the chosen item should have some basic value to you in order to achieve the desired effect.

I know this is a very direct challenge and it may seem like a lot to ask, but you are at an important crossroads.

What is more important, really? Do you want to hold onto this one possession now and forever, or challenge yourself to achieve a new way of thinking that will ensure your long-term success?

By actively letting go of something you consider meaningful, you will be allowed the opportunity to feel firsthand that *it's not that bad.*

By getting this out of the way now, you will build the confidence you need to repeat this process in the business world on a regular basis. Not to mention, you will raise some capital in the process, which might even get you out of reading Chapter 3!

I went through this process myself. There was a time when I thought I would never sell my old guitar amplifier. It had sentimental value, including personal experiences attached to it that could "never be replaced."

Furthermore, I knew that, if I ever sold this guitar amp, I would only net a little more than $100 from the sale, so why throw away all those great memories for a small handful of $20 bills?

What I eventually discovered was that the guitar amplifier was holding me back. This particularly heavy amplifier was taking up space, not being used, and was begging to be converted into cash to put into my next deal.

Ultimately, I sold it for $140 to someone who could not have been more excited about it. It went to a good new home, and it freed up valuable cash for reinvestment on my end. This reinvestment eventually led me to my new and improved guitar amplifier, a top of the line, hand-wired amp that retails for over $5,000.

Do you think I regret selling my old amplifier? Of course not. Now it's your turn to let go and move forward with your success.

2. Face Your Fears

Facing your fears is not an easy thing to do. It is not easy for me, or for you, or for anyone. However, it is something we frequently *must* do if we wish to go beyond our current state of living and achieve something greater.

The way this usually manifests in resale situations is through a *fear of purchasing*.

Maybe you don't know exactly how much you can resell an item for, so you hesitate to buy it; or maybe you do know how much you can sell it for, but you are not sure how long it will take, so you walk away from the deal.

How can we move past this limiting mindset?

Moving forward begins with understanding how this fear reaction originates in the first place.

Deep down, we humans perceive failure as "bad" and try to avoid it by not taking risks. The primitive part of us that cares about survival on an evolutionary level knows that if we do not try, then we will not be able to fail.

As it turns out, this is just our inner croc brain trying to reach out and put the brakes on things before we encounter imaginary harm; and although this fear response helped us avoid life-threatening danger thousands of years ago, in modern society it does little more than hold us back. Uncertainty *should* give us pause to calculate our risk, but the fear response itself should not prevent us from taking action.

Realize: we must take risks in order to succeed at a high level. We frequently must make tough decisions without complete certainty of the outcome.

This means there must come a day where you take some hard-earned cash out of your wallet and invest in your first inventory item. This might seem risky or scary at the present moment, but it is the only way forward.

Understand that even if you wind up upside down on a few deals, by putting yourself out there and buying up some inventory, you will develop confidence in your abilities. Moreover, you can and will learn important lessons from your occasional failures.

For those of you who are still feeling unsure, consider this: even when I have wound up upside down on a deal myself, it was never that bad. I broke even on a handful of deals and ended up losing a little cash on another handful. But in using my valuation methods, believe it or not, to date I've never lost more than $40 in value on a single resale transaction.

How to Face Your Fears

As with the last exercise, this is optional. If you have already experienced financial loss in business, you can probably skip this because you already understand the concept. However, if you have not experienced loss, or believe you will struggle to make acquisitions (invest money) out of fear, this exercise can help you move past this potential road block.

Note that both this exercise and the previous one are designed around *exposure treatment* principles of behavioral therapy, in which a person's phobic response gradually extinguishes itself when the subject learns the target stimulus does not produce the harm originally feared.

Onto the exercise, then.

Buy something on Craigslist, then purposely mark it down and sell it at a small loss. Yes, you read that right. For the sake of this exercise, keep your losses to an absolute minimum, so I don't have to feel too bad for pushing you into this.

"But... WHAT?!" you say.

Yeah, I know. To reassure you, this book *is* about making money.

This exercise is meant to push you out of your comfort zone. It will prove to you that, even in failure, the sun will still rise tomorrow. At the end of the day, you will get most of your money back and realize it's not the earth-shattering event you once thought it was.

This is especially crucial if you have never experienced something like this before, because loss is bound to happen at some point in your ongoing business operations, and you do not want it to emotionally derail you when it does.

Once you have completed this exercise, instead of internally exclaiming, *"But... WHAT?!"* and having *that* reaction, you will be more calm in the event a particular deal does go south at some point in the future. Your confidence will remain intact and your emotions unaffected, even if there is a lesson to be learned.

Remember, this is a purely optional exercise and you are more than welcome to skip it for practical purposes. However, just be sure you are mentally and emotionally prepared to invest, and for the occasional speed bump that is bound to come up from time to time.

I have seen too many people fail to invest their money into great deals due to an irrational fear of loss. They sit there and mull a deal over, and while it kind of sounds good... ultimately they cannot bring themselves to take the risk. Interestingly, it is this lack of action that absolutely guarantees failure, whereas taking a chance provides an opportunity for success.

An Extra Note on Loss Aversion

As a final note on this subject, whether in relation to a fear of losing money (when purchasing) or inventory (when selling), everyone experiences a fear of loss to some degree. In psychology, this is termed **loss aversion** and it has a very real, measurable effect on the human psyche. In fact, this applies directly to both of the sections we have covered above – conquering your possessive nature and facing your fears.

The essence of loss aversion is that we all have a strong tendency to prefer avoiding losses to realizing gains. Daniel Kahneman and Amos Tversky were the first psychological researchers to clearly show this trend through tests conducted in the late 1970's. Several experiments have been done since then showing how loss aversion plays into human behavior and financial markets.

In the *Journal of Economics Perspectives* (Vol. 5, No. 1, 1991), Daniel Kahneman, Jack Knetsch, and Richard Thaler published an article titled "Anomalies: The Endowment Effect, Loss Aversion, and Status Quo Bias." The article cites several studies, including one conducted at Cornell University using students from an advanced economics class split into two groups. Group A was given coffee mugs and told they were theirs to keep. Group B was simply shown the same set of coffee mugs, and then they were taken away.

After a short time, each group was asked to place a value on the mugs. When asked to specify a price they would be willing to sell their mugs for, Group A's median owner asked $5.25. Yet the median buyer from Group B was willing to pay no more than $2.25-2.75! The experiment was performed over and over again, and it consistently resulted in median selling prices roughly *twice* as high as median buying prices.

Why was there such a large gap between prices?

It was concluded the primary factor responsible for the gap was a reluctance to sell. Specifically, selling prices were found to be higher due to the **endowment effect**, which states the psychological effects of loss aversion take hold when we experience a sense of ownership over something. In this case, the sellers wanted more money to justify the additional pain that came with giving up mugs that were now *theirs*.

Notice the effects of endowment do not lead to an increase in the inherent appeal of an item, but rather an *increase in the pain* associated with letting it go. This increased pain is what leads to the assignment of a higher price, thought to justify these feelings – even if an ideal outcome exists at a lower selling price.

Moving back to our subject matter, this is why *seeing Craigslist transactions as a business* (rather than seeing them as personal transactions) is so powerful, since it helps you move you away from the clouded decision-making that is so common due to our innate psychological makeup.

By mentally separating your *personal* assets from your *business* assets in your mind, you can come to view your business activities through a more rational frame of mind. Your personal sense of attachment does not into play quite as much when your business is viewed as a separate, independent entity apart from your personal affairs.

Viewed through this lens, neither the fear of losing *money* when investing in new inventory, nor the fear associated with losing an *item* itself during a sale, is quite as significant. In turn, this emotional freedom enables you to act faster and with more confidence when making ongoing business decisions, ultimately reaching higher levels of success in shorter periods of time.

For additional reading on this subject, I would highly recommend an article titled "When Do Losses Loom Larger than Gains?" by Dan Ariely, Joel Huber, and Klaus Wertenbrauch from the *Journal of Marketing Research*(May, 2005). Notably, it is explained how the endowment effect may be circumvented when in a "selling frame of mind," as opposed to an "endowment state of mind." This is at the essence of seeing Craigslist transactions from a business perspective.

It is notable that you can leverage loss aversion to your advantage as a seller by literally putting an item into a potential buyer's hands. Virtually every retailer uses this psychology to their advantage, since once a person holds something in their own two hands, tries it on, or otherwise uses it, their sense of attachment starts taking root and increases the threshold price they are willing to pay – to avoid *losing* the item now in their hands.

Think about the many forms this comes in: software demos, free trials, test drives, trying clothes on, product samples... how many times have you bought something after "testing it out" that you never would have bought beforehand? How many times did you pay a higher price than you would have originally been willing to pay?

As a seller, I generally have my potential buyers try out an item during our meeting *before* asking for payment, even though the price is almost always negotiated beforehand. This provides buyers with an opportunity to honestly evaluate the item they have come to purchase. But it also helps "seal the deal" by creating a sense of ownership and thus represents the correct logical order of events. Demo first, payment last.

3. Learn a Useful NLP Trick

Before we move onto the next chapter, I want to share a Neuro-Linguistic Programming (NLP) trick with you that I learned back in college.

Feel free to skip over this if you'd like, but if you enjoyed the first part of this chapter, you will probably enjoy this next exercise as well.

This NLP trick is a powerful way to immediately shift your focus and control your perceptions of the various experiences you have in life. I have tailored it to be quick and easy to implement, so it can be used on the fly just about anywhere if you have two or three minutes to sneak away (to a bathroom, perhaps) and close your eyes.

Performing this trick will force you to stay focused on the good, positive things that you seek and help you avoid dwelling on the negatives we all must face from time to time. Use this trick whenever you need a mental or emotional boost to shift your mind back to your true goals. It is easy to get hung up on the little stuff sometimes; this will pull you out of the weeds and "reset" your mind and mood.

Here is some background to help you understand the purpose of the exercise.

When we perceive things to be important to us, whether they are past, present, or future events, we tend to blow them up very large in our minds.

We see these things in full color, and they may even play back to us like videos. We hear sounds, smell smells, and so on, being totally immersed as a character in our mental creation using all five senses. This amplifies any emotions we feel, too, because we make it so real for ourselves.

On the other hand, when we perceive something to be relatively unimportant, we quickly file it away in the back of our mind.

It might not be a full-color video, either, but instead a small and insignificant snapshot in black and white. After enough time, details are difficult to recall, because we did not conjure up anything extravagant in our minds when initially forming the memory of the event.

Now I must pose a question to you.

Would it not be fantastic if you could remember the many good, positive, and successful things that occur in your life in full HD, while simultaneously quickly "filing away" less exciting, non-productive things as small black-and-white snapshots, soon to be forgotten? Would it not be great if your mind was trained to generally focus more on the positive things and quickly let the negatives roll off your back?

Yes!

Fortunately, there is a specific mental process that anyone can do from their alert, conscious mind-state that will influence and "reprogram" their subconscious in an intentional manner. This is how it works:

Part A: Strengthening Positives

1. First, find a relaxing and quiet place to perform this exercise. The exercise can be done in more distracting environments, but for your first time, you should be somewhere that you can give your full attention to it.
2. Think of something good that happened to you recently, within the past week. It might be a major life event, or it might be something extremely small, like finding a good parking spot at the grocery store.
3. Evaluate your first impression of the memory. Is it easy to recall what happened? Are you viewing your memory as a full color, full HD video in your mind, or is it more of a snapshot?
4. Now you are going to reconstruct the memory into a highly detailed HD video. Walk yourself through the memory, starting with what you were doing immediately beforehand. Look at yourself from a distance in the third person as the picture comes into focus. Then walk through the rest of the memory until its completion.
5. Throughout the process, make sure you are seeing all of the colors around you, and blow up the video image in your mind as big as you can make it.
6. Go through the rest of your five senses in detail, remembering what it physically *felt* like, what it *smelled* like, all the *sounds* you heard, and the *taste*, if there was one. Recall the *emotions* you felt in vivid detail, too. Focus

intently on how great the things are that are happening in your memory.

7. Finally, step into your character (remove yourself from the third person perspective and put yourself into the first person) and fully immerse yourself in the memory as though it was happening again in real life. Stay here for a few minutes and absorb as much as you can.

8. When the memory is as vivid as possible, you are ready to *anchor* it in your mind. In order to anchor it, open up an imaginary briefcase and stuff this memory into it.

9. The more detail you include about the briefcase itself, the better. How big is it and what color is it? Maybe it has a scratch on the corner, and perhaps you need to use a special code to open it. Making the briefcase unique helps you create a mental pathway that you can trigger each time you store your positive memories.

10. From here forward, you will tend to remember this memory in more detail and with more positive emotion. Furthermore, if you are ever having a bad day or need to perk yourself up, you can quickly place yourself back in this mindset by taking out your imaginary briefcase, unlocking it, and pulling your memory out of it again.

Part B: Minimizing Negatives

1. Like in Part A, find a relaxing and quiet place to perform this exercise.

2. Think of something undesirable that happened to you recently, within the past week. Again, this could be anything from a major life event to a very small or petty setback.

3. Evaluate your first impression of the memory. Is it easy to recall what happened? Are you viewing your memory as a full color, full HD video in your mind, or is it more of a snapshot?

4. Now you are going to deconstruct the memory into an extremely small, insignificant black-and-white photo. Regardless of the level of detail you originally remember, you

will be removing details one by one until there is almost nothing left.

5. First, take yourself out of the first person in your memory and place yourself at a far, far distance in the third person. You are looking at yourself in this situation from very far away as a neutral observer.

6. Next, dumb down the mental movie into a mere single-shot photograph of the experience. Once you have this singular picture in mind, make it grayscale (black and white) and detach yourself from any emotion or feeling that previously existed. As a third party observer, the feelings gradually slip away until they are no longer there.

7. Remove any other senses you may have associated with this experience. There are no smells, no sounds, no tastes...nothing. Just that one-frame visual snapshot that is now in grayscale and shrinking quickly. Shrink the photo down in your mind to the point where you almost can't see it anymore; it should be smaller than your fingernail.

8. When this memory has been stripped down, made void of any emotion, and shrunk as much as possible, you are ready to anchor it in your mind in that format. In order to anchor it, open up an imaginary trash can and throw away the picture.

9. Like with the briefcase in Part A, the more detail you include about the trash can itself, the better. How big is it and what color is it? Is it made out of metal, plastic, or what? Is there a can liner inside? Making the trash can unique helps you create a mental pathway that you can trigger each time you discard your negative memories.

10. From here forward, you will tend to forget about this memory. When you do recall it, the memory will seem much less significant and important than it originally was, like it does not really matter or affect you.

For best results, I would recommend picking a handful of significant emotional events to work through in Part A (positive associations), and then another handful of events to walk through in Part B (negative disassociations).After just fifteen minutes of going through these exercises, you will be amazed how excited you are about the many positive things going on in your life, and quite surprised at how the things you had been dwelling on just don't matter anymore.

Furthermore, there are three specific applications for these NLP exercises in our case: conquering loss aversion, managing your emotions after failures, and constructing a fiercely tough belief system capable of ignoring negative outside influences.

To conquer loss aversion, imagine yourself in a buying or selling situation in your mind's eye. Let your emotional attachment and fears related to loss aversion come to the surface, and then address these feelings with Part B of the exercise, minimizing the emotional significance related to such events. Then, follow this up with an imaginary success scenario and bring it to life in your mind using Part A. This will strengthen your resolve to buy and sell objectively, and minimize emotional resistance to making otherwise sound business and sales decisions.

To manage your emotions after a failure, loss, or other setback, simply go through Part B to minimize what I like to call the "post-traumatic effects" of such an experience. This can be very powerful as an ongoing maintenance measure; you do not want the occasional and inevitable setback to create undue emotional resistance to taking reasonable business risks in the future. Plus, having a systematic process like this to address the occasional failure means there is less to fear at the outset of a new risk; even if you do fail, you already have a plan to quickly address such an occurrence and move on, as opposed to getting caught up in an emotional loop of self-doubt and confusion.

Finally, to construct a fiercely tough belief system, think of a time someone important to you said something negative about your abilities. Surely none of us are so blessed to have 100% positive people surrounding us; even the best spouses, brothers, sisters, parents, and children can get stressed out and say things that damage our self-confidence, whether or not that is their intention. Imagine this person standing in front of you and listen to them saying their negative remark while looking you in the eye. Then, using Part B, reduce this full-color mental "video" down to something very small and insignificant. Rinse and repeat a few times if necessary, and be sure to use this to disarm all of the negative people in your life.

Next, you should recount the times people have complimented you or said things to boost your confidence, and run through Part A with those to amplify their effect in your mind. Note that the more often you run through these exercises, the better equipped you will be to let the positive people in your life support you while simultaneously putting up an impenetrable mental barrier to those who are not.

Even though this third application of our NLP exercises may initially seem unrelated to the subject matter of this book, I include it for an important reason: as you get into buying and reselling things on Craigslist, you may encounter people who do not believe in your abilities or who are jealous of your success, and who wish to discourage you. With this tool, you can easily program your mind to effectively ignore them as you advance further down the road of success. It is important to have a tool like this to *functionally* ignore negative influences at a mental and emotional level, as opposed to simply pretending to ignore them at a social level. Pretending is great for appearances, but does little to help us on the inside, where it really matters.

Chapter 2 Recap

- Let go of your possessive nature by learning to see items as *business inventory*.
- Confidently face your fears and accept that failure is a powerful learning tool to be embraced.
- Create a separate compartment in your mind for your business finances and related decisions.
- Use NLP exercises to conquer loss aversion, manage your emotions, and build a fiercely tough belief system capable of rejecting negative outside influences.

Top performers know that a bulletproof mind is the first step toward achieving great things.

By replacing limiting thought patterns and viewpoints with more effective, positive ways of thinking, you can achieve almost anything. Challenge yourself to change your beliefs and outlook by taking action now and putting yourself through the exercises laid out in this chapter. This will make you mentally tough and provide hard evidence that you are ready for the periodic ups and downs of the business world.

Assignments

1. Practice one or more exercises from this chapter to sharpen your mind.

On Deck

In the next chapter, we will discuss seven different ways you can raise capital to get started with buying and reselling merchandise on Craigslist. These are "guerilla" strategies anyone can implement to raise capital, even when living paycheck to paycheck

3

RAISE CAPITAL

HOW I TURNED A FREE ITEM INTO $500

This chapter will give you the tools you need to raise seed money for your new business. When getting off the ground, there are certain concessions you may need to make that conflict with the other principles in this book. Do not worry about this; raising capital is a one-time event that warrants making exceptions to certain rules.

Preparation
Planning & Measuring
Deal Analysis
Purchasing
Sales

For example, I do not advocate driving all over town to make deals, whether you are buying or selling, once your business is up and running. However, when you are raising capital, it is perfectly acceptable to do this.

Perhaps you find a piece of furniture on the free section of the listings that you know you can resell for $40-50. By all means, go grab it and get to selling. You will net less than $40-50 after subtracting your gas and time from the transaction, but nonetheless, this can give you the cash you need to start purchasing and reselling.

That being said, you might have an easier way to gather up $100, $250, or even $500 to invest in this new side business of yours. Perhaps you can afford to take some money out of your paycheck or savings account, for instance. If this describes you, then you can skip most of this chapter and move on to Chapter 4. Make sure to read the part below about using the free section of Craigslist, though, because I have a good story there for you. In fact, I have two good stories for you, as well as some information on staying safe that is very important.

On the other hand, if funds are tight and you can barely scrape together money for dinner tonight, do not worry; you still have some options. Let's look at seven ways you can get into the game, even if you are starting from $0.00.

1. Start with the Free Section
2. Sell Things You Already Own
3. Give Up Something Temporarily
4. Do Freelance Work on Fiverr or Elance
5. Pick Up an Extra Shift
6. Broker a Deal
7. Borrow from a Friend or Family Member

1. Start with the Free Section

Before you discount picking up free stuff as a viable method for raising capital, let me give you a powerful reason to listen up.

Simply put, the most profitable deal I have ever done was something I got from the free section.

At some point in my quest to learn about buying and selling things on Craigslist, I started getting crazy ideas like, *"What if people are giving away really valuable stuff?"* and *"How cool would it be if I could pick something up for free and turn it into serious cash!"*

Like most people, and probably not unlike yourself, I had plenty of doubts. "That's never going to happen" and "If it's too good to be true, it probably is" frequented my thoughts.

Nonetheless, there was a fire burning inside me and I was determined to find *something* of value to pick up and resell from the free section. Before long, I found it.

<u>My Most Profitable Deal Ever</u>

It was a church organ in alright condition, and the gentleman who had it listed on the free section had kept it in his garage for the past ten to fifteen years, after it was removed from a church. He was tired of storing it and didn't want to deal with the hassle of it anymore. It required lots of help to move, and was not being put to any use. More importantly, he really needed the space in his garage for another purpose, and it would have actually cost him money to hire someone to remove and dispose of it.

After confirming a meeting time with him, I called up the drummer in my band to help me load and move this beast.

We drove down to the Point Loma area of San Diego together and backed into the seller's driveway. His garage door was open, and I remember looking at how much dust had accumulated on the surface of the organ. It was insane.

The bench that came with it was in terrible shape, visibly delaminating on top. The seller did have the original foot pedals, case, paperwork, warranty, and everything else that came with the organ originally, though, and it sounded alright when tested.

It took some real effort to load this thing into my truck!

Above is a picture of the organ loaded up in my truck, strapped down and ready for the drive back. When we finally got back to our recording studio, it was looking like it'd be a real pain getting this behemoth up the stairs to the second floor.

Fortunately, the other guys in my band showed up for practice about the same time we started unloading the organ. Between the four of us, we were able to get it up after a healthy effort.

Here's a good picture of the organ once it was in place and I had a chance to clean it up with some Pledge. It took a couple hours to scrub every nook and cranny, but I knew getting it back into good shape was the right thing to do.

The Allen Organ is looking good after a clean-up session

We made some funny videos with the organ, each giving a poor attempt at playing it, and generally had a fun time with it for the next couple of months. I even considered just keeping the organ, since it was free and it added some real character to the studio.

But deep down, I always knew selling it was the right move, and we needed the extra space. Most of all, I needed to raise capital to sustain my side business.

There was something extra-motivating about selling this organ, too. When I cracked the bench open for the first time, I found the original price tag along with all the original paperwork. It listed an original sale price of $7,600 on the tag.

Wow

This was one of the few times that I had not previously researched the "new" price of an item before picking it up, and it came as a pleasant surprise. Obviously, it was not worth nearly what it used to be, since so many years had passed and it was worn, but it confirmed my suspicion that the resale would be meaningful.

It took several weeks to sell, though, even with this beautiful picture posted in my listing. A good three weeks or so went by without a single email from anyone expressing interest. As time went on, I went through a period of doubt as I considered the possibility that I wasgoing to be stuck with this extremely bulky organ for a long time. I reminded myself that patience is a virtue, though, and maintained confidence that it would eventually sell.

Finally I got a couple emails from interested folks, and one guy even came to test it out, but ultimately decided it was not for him. He was a really good organ player, too! The organ really came to life when he played it.

After more time passed, I finally received an email from the eventual buyer.

To: 6jfcd-3952553640@sale.craigslist.org
Sent: Tuesday, August 6, 2013 11:06 AM
Subject: Allen Organ Model ADC 220 - $500 (San Diego)

Hello!

I am interested in your organ and would like to ask you several questions.

Is there any keys or pedals or stops that need to be repaired?

Does this organ have internal speakers?

I emailed her back and answered her questions. We exchanged a few more emails clarifying some details about the organ, and I clarified that her payment would need to be in cash (not check, which she had asked about). Speaking of which, make sure you *always deal in cash and nothing else.* This is a hard and fast rule.

When my potential buyer came out with her husband to test the organ, it was quite the ordeal. It took some time for her to go through all the different settings, look at everything in detail, and mull it over. She asked if I could lower the price at all, and I agreed to take $50 off my asking price.

We made the deal, and she sent her husband off to get a U-Haul truck to load and transport the organ back to her place, which was a long ways away. My bass player and I helped them load it into the U-Haul, and the husband was so grateful that he paid me the full $500 in the end. I think he felt bad because they had agreed ahead of time to bring their own help to move it, but ended up relying on us. After all, it was an unexpected half-hour of legitimately backbreaking work for the two of us.

At the end of the day, the extra and unexpected work was well worth it. I started with an item I acquired for free and turned it into $500 cash! There are other deals out there that require much less effort and have the potential to net just as much cash, so do not think that you need to own a truck or be in great physical condition to do this. It simply requires some periodic browsing of the free listings and the ability to quickly respond to fresh listings that show promise.

In fact, almost every time I browse the free listings, there's at least one item that can be resold for $20-25. Sometimes I'll even find nice furniture, musical instruments, and other valuables that could be sold for $100 or more, including the occasional gem like the organ I found. Most of these can be transported in a regular car and would require very little effort to lift, transport, and store.

The free listings can be a gold mine, not to mention a case in point of *"one man's trash is another man's treasure."* If you put just a little time and patience into them, you can quickly build up a few hundred dollars that can be used to kick-start your business. After that, you may even want to continue browsing the free listings periodically once you're up and running!

Now let's look at another great story that illustrates how starting with nothing can turn into something significant.

The Red Paperclip Story

If you really want to knock yourself out, grab a cold one and set aside a good hour to read Kyle MacDonald's blog: http://oneredpaperclip.blogspot.com/

Spoiler alert: Kyle started off with one red paperclip, made a series of trades, and wound up with a house. Yes, a *house.* He covers the entire story and the trades he made in explicit detail on his web site, and it is really quite an impressive story. This guy really understands value.

Here is a summary of the series of trades he made, beginning with the paperclip and ending with the house:

Red Paperclip	Fish Pen
Fish Pen	Doorknob
Doorknob	Coleman Stove
Coleman Stove	Generator
Generator	Instant Party
Instant Party	Snowmobile
Snowmobile	Trip to Yahk
Trip to Yahk	Cube Van
Cube Van	Recording Contract
Recording Contract	One Year in Phoenix
One Year in Phoenix	Afternoon with Alice Cooper
Afternoon with Alice Cooper	Kiss Snow globe
Kiss Snow globe	One Movie Role
One Movie Role	503 Main Street

During one of his blog posts, Kyle discusses the importance of **relative value**. This was in reference to a question about why he would trade an afternoon with Alice Cooper for what might seem like a silly snow globe. Well, Kyle knew it was a unique snow globe, and knew that to the right person it carried more value than one might imagine. Of course, he eventually exchanged the snow globe for the movie role that was directly traded for the house.

Everyone has different perceptions of value, including you, so stay positive and do not make any assumptions that what you have will not sell or is not worth a lot to somebody else. The organ I sold is another good example of this. It took some time, and I had to be patient, but eventually a buyer came along who could appreciate its value.

Working the Free Listings

If I could pick up a free organ and turn it into $500 cash, and Kyle MacDonald could turn a red paperclip that he already had into a house, I know in my heart that you can raise a little money by trading or reselling free stuff, too.

Even if it's not $500 or a house on your first try, I am absolutely certain you can scrape together a few hundred bucks this way, which is more than enough to get started. There is plentiful low-hanging fruit available all the time in the free section.

In fact, during my own start-up phase, I started out by sourcing a handful of lower-value free items for resale. I picked up some furniture and appliances that turned into an extra couple hundred dollars in the beginning, before my organ deal.

People give away nice end tables, coffee tables, decorations, lamps, kitchen appliances, and other things that you can pick up even if you only have a regular car. If you *do* have a truck and a place to store larger items, there are more free couches, chairs, and coffee tables available than you might think.

As a case in point, here is a screen shot (as of the time of this writing) of the free section showing a mirror, bed frame, piano, file cabinet, BBQ, and a handful of couches.

Two free Mirrors - (rancho bernardo) pic map

Free Sealy Posturepedic Queen Box Spring - (Oceanside) pic

Working antique Bradbury piano - (Oceanside, CA) pic

Free Sofa and Love Seat - (carlsbad ca) pic map

Wooden bed frame - (carlsbad) pic

Concrete - (San Carlos / Allied Gardens / Del Cerro) pic map

File cabinet - (carlsbad) pic

Free chairs - pic

Sofa for FREE, Clare model from Macy's, sage green - (La Jolla) pic

Free fill dirt (delivered) - (San Diego)

donate your blankets - (chulavista)

free fire wood 2 cords - (vista) map

Free BBQ Grill - (Mission Beach) map

FREE FILL DIRT - (rancho santa fe) pic

Free Couch - (Mission Valley) pic

These are just the first ten or so listings that appear right now on my screen, and already I can see that the mirrors, BBQ grill, file cabinet, bed frame, and couch could be resold for $20 each, if not more. You could easily put together a good $60 or more right there. Not to mention the antique piano, which has the potential to be like my organ deal, representing several hundreds of dollars in profit.

In case you're wondering, I did check the pictures on these listings and everything looked good. Generally speaking, a lot of stuff in the free section is *not* in the best shape, but if you keep your eye on the listings, eventually you will find stuff in decent enough condition to resell.

Speaking of looking fine, check out this leather couch that was just a few more listings down:

Free black leather couch (Hillcrest/Univeristy Heights)

This couch is in impeccable shape, and I have seen others like it go for $200-300 in the for-sale listings.

Now, check out this listing from a different geographic location!

This person is actually offering to *pay* $10 just to have someone come pick up their couch and remove it from their home. It's not as nice as a black leather couch, but it could still be sold for $15-30 to the right buyer. On top of the $10 removal fee the owner is paying, this could easily be a $25-40 resell.

By the way, for you truck owners out there: couches and other large items are more difficult for the average person to pick up, so there is less competition. As long as you are not contacting someone who posted their listing several days ago, there is a good chance that you will be the first person to express interest and have the ability to follow through. When I started out, I picked up three couches for free and generated a little more than $100 by reselling them.

I also picked up a really nice leather couch for my own house in absolutely mint condition for $100 that originally cost $900 new at M or Furniture. It looks like it came right off the showroom floor, and if the time comes that I ever need to resell it, I can promise you I will get at least $200.

A Note on Safety

As a last note on picking up free stuff, *please be careful.* I have never had an issue in any of my dealings, nor have I known anyone who has run into an uncomfortable situation, so the odds are in your favor.

Still, you must take every precaution to stay safe when dealing with strangers. This is true for your ongoing business dealings as well. There is no way around meeting with other people if you are starting a Craigslist business, and this is something you need to accept up front if you are serious about transacting business on a regular basis with folks from local classified ads. However, if you keep some basic safety tips in mind, you can go about your business with minimal concern.

- Bring a friend or family member with you if you are venturing out into unfamiliar territory or are unsure of your own ability to stay safe.
- Talk to the other party on the phone ahead of time to give yourself a chance to notice anything out of the ordinary in their speech or personality.
- Ask to meet in a public place if possible, and set up your deals during daylight hours, as opposed to late at night.
- Make sure you have a charged cell phone in case it becomes necessary to phone for help.
- Park your vehicle in a place where it will be easy to drive away if you need to leave in a hurry, and consider bringing pepper spray if you feel the slightest bit of discomfort.
- Do not wear anything that will draw extra attention to yourself, and pay extra attention to your surroundings when you arrive.
- Should anything seem out of the ordinary upon your arrival, leave immediately.

We will briefly touch on safety again later on, but these are some general guidelines that you can implement now for maximum peace of mind.

To conclude our discussion on generating cash with free items, I would challenge you to look at the free listings right now and begin contacting folks who have nice things you could pick up in the immediate future. Even if you don't need the money, it still might be fun to go through this process. This is an easy, off-the-cuff way for anyone to drum up a little extra cash in a pinch.

Now let's look at the next way you can raise capital for your new business.

2. Sell Things You Already Own

If you already have valuable things you can afford to part with, this is the quickest and most straightforward way to go about raising money. As much as I might advocate turning free stuff into cash, selling off stuff around the house is more efficient.

During the seven month period of time in which I made several thousand dollars with my system, I sold quite a few things I already had in order to free up more funds. I knew if I could inject more money into more inventory, more profitable sales would be just around the corner. Getting rid of old stuff really felt great, too.

The basic process here is really simple. Take high-quality photos of your stuff (like you always should, since a picture can make or break a sale before it even happens – see Chapter 10 for more on this), figure out what you should price it at, and get it listed. Then prepare to answer emails and set up times to meet buyers.

When selling the acoustic guitar I had owned for ten years, it was not easy. I was emotionally attached, like we discussed in the last chapter. The funny thing is, when I sold it, I wasn't even at a point where I really needed the additional funds to invest. However, I had learned to not be emotional and was eager to inject more cash into my existing pool of funds, purchase more inventory, and keep the cycle going at an even faster pace.

Here is an old picture of that guitar:

My 1st Seagull S6 Acoustic Guitar

Was my decision worth it? You tell me. Here is the series of buys/sells I went on to make after getting $330 for the sale of my original guitar.

$330 received for my original Seagull S6 acoustic guitar w/hard case
$225 invested in another Seagull S6 acoustic guitar w/hard case (we'll call this Seagull #2)
$340 received for the sale of Seagull #2
$315 invested in the purchase of a Taylor 110 Acoustic Guitar w/hard case
$425 received for the sale of the Taylor w/hard case
$160 invested in the purchase of a left-handed Seagull S6 acoustic w/hard case
$295 received for the sale of the left-handed Seagull w/hard case
------
Total: $690
Net Gain: $360

My net gain is calculated by subtracting the original $330 I started with by selling my original guitar. Notably, by the end of all this, I could have bought back my original guitar at the exact price I sold it for and still had an additional $360 in my pocket. Instead, I took the entire $690 and reinvested it into additional inventory purchases that turned into additional profit down the line.

This example demonstrates how selling something you currently own can be a powerful way to raise capital for your new business. It may feel like you are parting with something meaningful or important in the beginning, but the benefits have excellent potential to greatly outweigh the immediate loss in the long run.

Now it is your turn to think long and hard about things of value you might be willing to part with in order to raise capital for yourself. If you completed your assignment in Chapter 2 by selling something you own to let go of your possessive nature, you may have already raised some decent funds this way.

3. Give Up Something Temporarily

This method might not be for everyone, but if you are willing to make some temporary sacrifices to set aside extra money, it can be a relatively easy way to raise capital that does not require much time or involvement.

Think about your budget and expenses for a minute.

Is there some area of life you could cut back on, even temporarily, to save up a couple hundred bucks to get this project off the ground?

If so, this is yet one more viable way to get going. Maybe you give up beer for a month, pass on that next concert ticket, or put off buying a new pair of jeans. Heck, you could even eat Ramen for a few weeks to save money, like so many of us did back in college. You get the idea. For motivation, remind yourself that, whatever you might give up for a short period of time now, you will gain back much more in the end.

Here are some simple ideas to put this into action:

- Save on gas by driving less for a few weeks.
- Save on food by sticking to a strict grocery-only budget for a month or two.
- Put off buying extra clothes or non-essential items for a while.
- Eliminate or cut back on a vice like smoking or drinking.
- Avoid going out to shows or other costly events.
- Temporarily refrain from buying anything you do not really need.

The nice thing is that it does not take much to get started besides a little self-discipline. Even if you can free up a measly hundred bucks, you can turn that into $150 or $200 pretty quickly and then you are off to the races.

I understand this can be extra difficult when living paycheck to paycheck. Believe me, I have been there myself. It was never easy, but I always got through it. Anyone can make it work with the right attitude.

4. Do freelance work on Fiverr or Elance

Do you have a skill that you could charge money for on the side?

Both www.Fiverr.com and www.Elance.com provide online marketplaces for work-for-hire arrangements. What this means is that you can hire people to do things for you through the site, or alternatively be one of the contractors available for hire by others.

In your scenario, you would be signing up as a contractor to work for someone else. If you browse through these sites for a good fifteen minutes, you will get a long list of ideas of how you might contribute.

People with photoshop skills edit pictures for people. Writers compose articles or do editing work. People with large social followings post links to their audiences on social media platforms for a small fee. The list goes on.

I have sold a few gigs on Fiverr myself and generated some decent extra cash in my free time, so I know it is easy enough to do. Likewise, Elance has an easy process for both contractors and vendors to follow.

Once you setup an account, it is just a matter of time before you get some business. For anyone who needs some extra cash on the side, it is certainly worth exploring.

As a bonus freelance idea, for those of you living in cities where Lyft and Uber are active and condoned, you might consider driving for these services in your free time. By doing this, a decent chunk of change can be earned in no time. Just be sure your locale does not impose restrictions on these services, as some areas do.

5. Pick up An Extra Shift at Work

Not everyone works for an hourly wage at a job with flexible schedules, but if you do, picking up a few extra shifts can get you the money you need to get rolling with your new business.

In my own experience doing shift work, the easiest way to get an extra shift is to talk a co-worker into letting you cover for them. Alternatively, you can express interest in picking up some extra hours to your boss or scheduling manager.

6. Broker a Deal

Brokering is one of the more exciting avenues of Craigslist, in my humble opinion. The principle here is that you sell something that you do not own yet. Then, once you sell it, you go out and buy it at a cheaper price than you sold it for. In order to do this, you need to be a buyer and seller at the same time. Let me explain.

For example, let's say you see a Widget for sale on Craigslist for $250. You email the seller, and after negotiating, he agrees that he would accept $175. At the same time, you put up your own listing for the same Widget and eventually find a buyer who is willing to pay $225.

At this point, you gain the $50 difference between the two prices. You will need to take some risk here by taking cash out of somewhere to pay the original seller before re-selling to your buyer, though, so this method is not for everyone. If the sales end of your deal does not go through for some reason, you will be out the money until you're able to sell the item you just purchased.

The nice thing about brokering is that, since you are buying and reselling at almost the same time, you do not sit on inventory. If nothing else, it is worth a thought and possibly a revisit once you get up and running with your operations.

If brokering seems too good to be true, just remember that most businesses operate along similar lines. In my professional career, much of my sales experience has been a form of brokering. The companies I have worked for practice just-in-time inventory, so the inventory typically is not sourced or produced until an order has been placed by the client.

7. Borrow from a Friend or Family Member

Last but not least, you can always ask a trusted friend or family member to lend you a couple hundred bucks.

Do not ask anyone who you think will not be entirely supportive of your entrepreneurship, though. In fact, the reason I put this as a last option is because it is something I would personally avoid if possible.

Asking to borrow someone's money might invite them to question your abilities or check in with you on a regular basis, which adds pressure that you do not need at this early stage. Furthermore, it creates a debt that might put a strain on the underlying relationship until it has been paid.

However, if you have the sort of relationship that makes it okay to ask someone for a favor like this, and you are confident they will support you, by all means feel free to ask. There is nothing wrong with asking for a favor from friends or family from time to time. Only you can know whether or not this is a good idea, though, so proceed with your best judgment.

Chapter 3 Recap

- Turn trash into treasure by leveraging free listings.
- Sell things you already own to raise capital fast.
- Do freelance work, pick up a shift, give something up temporarily, or broker a deal to generate extra funds.
- Borrow money from a trusted friend or family member if you must.

With so many ways to generate a little cash, I am absolutely certain you can do it in a short span of time once you set your mind to it. I have succeeded in applying all of these methods, and none of them were terribly difficult to tackle. You can easily raise $200, and much more, with these techniques; the key is to get up out of your chair and make it happen.

Assignments

1. Choose at least one method to raise capital and see it through to raise $200 or more.

On Deck

In the next chapter, we will review a key strategy to help you maximize your efforts, and ultimately your financial success, when transacting business on Craigslist. This strategy, and its underlying logic, should be understood at the beginning of your ventures, before you dive in and start buying or reselling.

4

PICK A NICHE

MAKE THIS ONE DECISION TO MAXIMIZE YOUR SUCCESS

This short chapter is all about *specializing* in one area. Over time, knowing a lot about a particular area will give you a huge edge in spotting deals and completing sales. Related to this is understanding how to efficiently scan sales listings, which we will cover in detail.

Preparation
Planning & Measuring
Deal Analysis
Purchasing
Sales

Realize that, in order to become extremely effective at both buying and reselling, you must have a niche. This is true regardless of your area of interest, and I really cannot stress this enough. You must be able to walk the walk, talk the talk, speak the lingo, and carry on a halfway intelligent conversation with someone about what you are selling (or buying!). More importantly, you need to understand variations between products and how those variations affect pricing. Personally, having played guitar for the better part of fifteen years, I've learned my way around music gear and have a bit of an eye for spotting deals now – this is my niche.

However, please do not think you need to invest something ridiculous like fifteen years learning your niche. The truth is that I have learned more about the *pricing* of musical equipment in the past year than in the first fourteen. This is because I started more actively researching, browsing, and reading about the various brands, makes, and models out there once I started purchasing items for resale.

Therefore, even though it may help if you start in a niche you are already very knowledgeable about, you do not need several years of experience in order to do this. You only need a willingness to learn a niche and stick to it. As you become more knowledgeable in that niche, your experience will start to guide you. Let me tell you a short story to illustrate how this works in practice.

How I Browse the Listings

Most days, I browse through the listings under the *Musical Instruments* section of Craigslist, and I filter it to show *Owner* listings only. This is because the *Dealer* listings are often bogus or spam my, and they tend to be full-price new items, which I am not trying to find or buy.

Sometimes I also like selecting a "view" that allows me to see thumbnails or full pictures of the listings, which is an option Craigslist provides. I use the regular text list view most of the time, though. This is because I can scroll through a larger number of listings quicker without being distracted by the flashy pictures people put up. Pictures are nice, but workflow efficiency is more important to me.

Searching by Category & Owner is Helpful Most of The Time

Last but not least, I will frequently click the *pic* box as well, to reflect that I only want to see listings that have pictures. This is true even if I am looking at the listings in text-only format. At the end of the day, I still need to make sure there will be an image for any listing(s) I actually click on and explore further.

After clicking the *search* button, my purpose is to scan the ads and identify deals. This means items that are already priced fairly low, so I would not need to lowball someone too badly to pay what I want to pay. Even better if I can find a deal *at* the listed price, which is less common but does happen from time to time. I jump on those quick, before anyone else can take advantage of them.

Other days, I have a specific item in mind that I would like to buy. Maybe it is something I would like to try out, review on my blog, or use at the studio for a while. In this case, I will just type in the name of what it is and look at all the listings that come up for it. Here is a search for "Les Paul" in the musical instruments section:

As you can see, the words "Les Paul" can mean different things to different people. There are Gibson and Epiphone brands, plus Standard, Classic, Traditional, and Pro variations of the Les Paul model. This is similar to how an automobile body style might be referred to as a "hatchback" or "coupe." Different auto makers all have their own versions, or brands, and any one auto maker's model may have variations – perhaps a "sport" version with a V8 engine, instead of a V6.

Of course, there is great value in understanding these seemingly subtle variations, as they generally represent dramatic differences in price and underlying value. Armed with the knowledge of these variations – and how they affect price and value – you will be well-equipped to analyze pricing for the items in your niche. Without this knowledge, however, you might open yourself up to additional risk, lest you accidentally compare apples and oranges.

To continue with our automotive example, consider this: Ford's GT Mustang with its V8 engine and premium upgrades is much more expensive than their base V6 model, so even though these are both Mustangs, their prices are worlds apart. They are really two completely different vehicles, despite sharing the Mustang name and a similar body style. You can imagine how important it is, then, to know which of the two you're looking at when buying, since these subtleties will affect your valuation – and the price you should pay. It would be a shame to buy a base, V6 model Mustang for the price of an upgraded GT, V8 model, but it could happen if you had the faulty belief that all Mustangs were the same.

Note that you will naturally acquire an understanding of such product variations with time, but you can accelerate the process by actively researching the products in your niche. Browsing manufacturer websites is a good place to start, and you can supplement that by joining an online forum or group devoted to your niche. In such forums and groups, you will typically find a number of experts and long-time hobbyists who share valuable information about niche products – information that cannot be easily found through a cursory web search. Beyond this, consider throwing in a magazine subscription for good measure, and follow a few established blogs or online news channels within your niche.

Getting "hooked in" to these various information sources is the key to gaining niche expertise, and does not require you to invest significant time getting up to speed. While I do spend some time outside of my Craigslist transactions reading up on niche products, most of the time I just accumulate information on the fly while browsing the listings. When I see a product of interest, I simply open up a few tabs in my internet browser and do some quick research on the spot. This is how I recommend you go about it, too. For any given product or group of products, this only takes minutes and can be very productive.

When you start scanning the listings, then, research some of the products you see listed for sale, and make an effort to figure out how the various brands and model designations affect price. Check manufacturer websites, any relevant user forums, and general web search results. As we will discuss in Chapter 6, you may also want to check secondary markets for relevant price information, such as eBay, the Craigslist results in nearby cities, and online retailers' sites.

This may seem like a lot of homework, but in reality it takes mere minutes and is a cornerstone to your success. The information you gain from this process is what allows you to make good purchasing decisions and ultimately be successful in turning inventory over for a profit. Be sure, then, to invest ample time in the beginning finding and bookmarking quality information sources, whether manufacturer websites, niche forums (you may even want to join and participate in one or two key forums), Facebook groups, industry blogs, relevant ecommerce websites, and any online secondary markets where used products in your niche are sold. In the long run, you will constantly be revisiting these places to do your research.

By the way, be patient with the research process when you are just starting out. In your first few weeks learning a niche, you may feel like a complete novice, but this will soon change. Over the course of time, you will see increasingly more products in the listings that you have already researched, boosting your confidence and making the deal-hunting process significantly more efficient as you continue to accumulate information.

Now, let me break down how I would think through the Les Paul listings shown above, given my current knowledge.

The first guitar listed, the Gibson Les Paul Studio, is overpriced at $900. Gibson *is* the more upscale brand, but Studio models are a stripped down version of the so-called real thing, which would be a Gibson Les Paul Standard or Gibson Les Paul Classic in this case. I have seen Gibson Les Paul Studio models listed recently for as low as $600, so this seller is just plain silly. In fact, in the same set of listings shown, you can see another Gibson LP listed for $650. Given this, who do you think is going to get more buyer inquiries – the guy asking $900 or the guy asking $650? Of course, the lower price will receive more purchase offers.

The next two guitars, both listed as Epiphone Les Paul Standards (one as a Pro model) are also a bit on the high side at $400 and $475. Epiphone is the inexpensive brand comparable to Gibson, much like Honda is to Acura or Toyota is to Lexus, and the price just isn't justified. In fact, these guitars typically go new for around $500, so to ask $475 for a used model is not reasonable. To go after this particular instrument, I would need to submit a fairly lowball offer (in the seller's eyes) to meet my target price for the acquisition. Note that I do submit low offers like this on the regular, but the likelihood of them being accepted is lower when asking prices are high.

Last but not least, in evaluating these listings – I know from personal experience that an Epiphone Les Paul Standard (or Classic) can be bought for around $200 without a hard case or $225 to $250 with a hard case. This is because I have done it five times myself.

Buy #1 - Epi LP Classic w/Hard Case @ $250
Buy #2 - Epi LP Std w/Hard Case @ $235
Buy #3 - Epi LP Std, no case @ $180
Buy #4 - Epi LP Std w/Hard Case @ $180*
Buy #5 - Epi LP Std, no case @ $200

*This was a great deal!

Similarly, I know they can be sold easily enough for $300 without a hard case or $350 with one, also speaking from personal experience.

Sell #1 - Epi LP Classic w/Hard Case @ $350
Sell #2 - Epi LP Std w/Hard Case @ $350
Sell #3 - Epi LP Std, no case @ $300
Sell #4 - Epi LP Std w/Hard Case @ $360
Sell #5 - Epi LP Std, no case @ $300

Bottom line, due to my niche experience (and in this case, personal sales history), I know there will be opportunities to buy at lower prices than the ones listed in this example, so those are the deals I will wait for – although it might be worth shooting a couple lowball offers to these sellers anyways. The worst they can say is no, right?

Still, my excitement will increase when I see folks listing their Les Paul guitars in the neighborhood of $300 or less, so I can make a lower offer that stands a better chance of being accepted. Then, as we have seen, I will turn around and consistently resell those guitars for a profit of approximately $100. This does require a little patience, but the wait isn't so bad given the money to be made.

To reiterate what I said earlier, be patient when getting started with a new niche. You will gain the sort of knowledge and experience shown in this example naturally over the course of time, so there's no need to stress simply because you don't have all the answers right now, today. Eventually, your increasing knowledge will allow you to identify more deals in less time, and give you additional confidence when investing and reinvesting funds in your business. What may start out feeling like "risky guesswork" will suddenly become a pattern that you can rinse and repeat time and again. As one profitable deal turns into another, you'll enter an upward spiral fueled by knowledge, efficiency, and experience.

A Note on Profit Maximization

Once you start buying and selling your first inventory items, you might feel a desire to pay back your initial investment as soon as possible. After all, it is natural to want to see money coming back in after it has gone out. However, unless you borrowed your initial investment from a loan shark, I recommend reinvesting your initial sales dollars back into your business to leverage the *multiplying effect*.

The *multiplying effect* is simple. Let's say you start your business today with $1,000 invested in your initial inventory. You then go on to resell this entire inventory for $1,500.

At this point, if you were to pay back your initial $1,000, you would need to start "all over again" with the $500 in profit you just made. If you realize the same profit margin on future deals (33.3% margin), it will take an additional 3 "flips" before you get back to $1,500 again:

$500→ $750
$750→ $1,125
$1,125→**$1,687**

On the other hand, what if you did three more "flips" continuing from the point of $1,500, at the same margin?

$1,500.00 → $2,250
$2,250.00 → $3,375
$3,375.00 →**$5,062**

As you can easily deduce, if you were to wait until *this* point to pay back the initial investment of $1,000, you would have $4,062 available for ongoing business operations, as compared to the $1,687total after paying back the investment sooner.

Of course, these numbers are purely theoretical, but the general principle still holds true. Early reinvestment allows greater multiplying and compounding to occur.

Along similar lines, leveraging **velocity of money** can lead to a profit multiplication of sorts. This is where you transact a higher volume of business at a lower profit margin to achieve greater overall profitability.

Imagine, for example, that you can choose between selling one item 1x/month for a $100 profit, or that same item 2x/month for a $75 profit per transaction. At the end of the month, selling the item twice yields $150 in profit as opposed to $100 on the single transaction.

The additional hassle, logistics, etc. of acquiring and selling the item twice might not make sense, depending on the situation, but in many cases it can lead to greater profitability and free up precious cash for reinvestment.

CHAPTER 4 RECAP

- Pick a niche to maximize your knowledge and identify more deals faster.
- Pick a niche you are already familiar with or legitimately interested in learning about.
- Get "hooked in" to quality information sources in your niche, such as manufacturer websites, niche forums Facebook groups, industry blogs, relevant ecommerce websites, and secondary markets outside of Craigslist.
- Buy and resell the same type of item a few times to get a handle on its real value.
- Spend less time on seller listings that are artificially inflated, and more time on those that are closer to your target purchase price.

Experience gives you valuable information to help you evaluate future deals. By starting in a niche and staying in that niche, you gain buying and selling experience that will only become more relevant and useful as you go along.

Assignments

1. Pick a niche!

   If something obvious does not come to mind, brainstorm three or four areas that you could potentially see yourself working in. Musical instruments, auto parts, collectibles, and antiques are just a few topics that come to mind.

   Look through some of the listings on Craigslist in those categories right now to get an idea of what you would be dealing with. Do additional research online to see what things are going for new and used on other web sites. Begin to wrap your mind around these markets, even if just on a cursory level, so you can determine exactly which one you will be most comfortable diving into.

On Deck

In the next chapter, we will learn the importance of setting ground rules for your Craigslist transactions. Additionally, we will look at some "big picture" financial organization tools that will help guide you over time. These things will serve as your compass as you navigate from one deal to the next.

5

SET A THRESHOLD

WHY I WALK IF THERE ISN'T AT LEAST $100 IN A DEAL

In this chapter, we will discover the importance of setting financial goals for your business. Primarily, you should have an earnings standard on a per-transaction basis that makes this project (or any business venture, for that matter) worth your precious time, energy,

Preparation
Planning & Measuring
Deal Analysis
Purchasing
Sales

and money. It's best to "set your threshold" up front, before you wind up knee-deep in things.

Setting Goals with a Profit Threshold

On a day-to-day basis, the easiest way to ensure your goals are being met is to set a "minimum profit target," or **profit threshold** for *all* of your deals, expressed in dollars (and not as a percentage). This is the minimum dollar amount that you aim to earn from all of your deals.

Heeding Your Profit Threshold as a Buyer

As a *buyer,* $100 is my profit threshold for any given deal. If there is not at least an estimated $100 in net profit in a deal, then I've learned it is simply not worth the bother to acquire a new item for resale, at least in my niche. In fact, for items with a value above $500 or so, my threshold moves up into the $150+ range.

The reasoning behind this is twofold.

First, I am not out to make pennies on these deals. You shouldn't be either. Remember, just as regular businesses operate with certain earnings standards, we too must work with earnings standards. Deals that fall below our profit threshold stop making sense, and may prolong the time and effort required to be successful.

Second, all the time you invest in researching listings, emailing people, and posting your own ads needs to be accounted for. If you are only aiming to make $20-25 on most deals, you will probably achieve nothing more than breaking even when you take into account your investment of time, even if you consistently hit your target profit on the sales side.

Therefore, as a *buyer*, you should always seek to acquire inventory based on your best guess that the eventual resale of an item will meet your profit threshold. Understand that sometimes you will not meet your target profit; this is exactly why it is so important to aim for a reasonable threshold number in the first place. A good target threshold will set you up on the purchasing side for the best possible outcomes on the sales side over time, even if you occasionally miscalculate.

On the purchasing side, then, we can say our profit threshold is a "hard" threshold, meaning we should adhere to the rule strictly (only snatching up deals when we believe we can earn at least our profit threshold on the sales side).

The only exception would be in a circumstance where you have an opportunity to pick something up at a very low price on which a great return can be realized. For instance, perhaps someone offers to throw an item into a deal for $20 that you are confident can be sold quickly for $40-60; in this circumstance, it would be hard to turn down "easy money." Still, these smaller deals should not be your main focus.

Heeding your Profit Threshold as a Seller

As a *seller*, we would also like to stick to our predefined profit threshold as much as possible. Importantly, though, there is more room to play with the threshold on the sales side. Taking a small dip below your threshold to keep inventory moving is almost always acceptable. In some cases, even taking a larger dip, breaking even, or suffering a small loss can be acceptable to clear a stale item (an item that has not sold for a long time) from inventory which is tying up valuable cash that could be reinvested elsewhere.

Therefore, on the sales side, we can say our profit threshold is a "soft" threshold, meaning we can more freely make exceptions to the rule when needed. Note that this is not *encouraged*, but acceptable if necessary. Typically, dipping below your established threshold will only be necessary if you have discovered your initial valuation was wrong, or when an item has been listed for so long that it makes sense to discount it, recoup the investment, and put it into something more profitable.

As a general rule of thumb, try not to break your profit threshold for at least three months after making a new acquisition, unless you get an offer so close to meeting your profit threshold that it makes sense to simply sell the item and move on. If, after three months, you get the sense that you have miscalculated the potential resale value, it might be time to make an exception and break the threshold.

In these cases, you might reduce your asking price, give a second chance to potential buyers whose offers you previously rejected, consider moving the product to a different market (Chapter 14), try to incorporate the item in a trade (Chapter 13), or redo the listing altogether with fresh pictures and a new description (listings that have been up forever can hurt the perceived value of your item, as "social proof" factors may cause someone to believe there is a reason no one else has bought your item).

In my own experience, I have often still been able to meet my profit threshold when employing one of these methods. In other cases, I have simply remained patient for the day when the right buyer does come around the bend.

Setting Your Profit Threshold

To reiterate, you want to adhere to your target profit threshold as much as possible. Let's get specific:

My profit threshold is $100 for any given deal, and I also knowmy average profit *margin*(note, profit margin is a different metric from profit threshold) at the present moment is around 34%. This means I should focus mostly on items that I can resell for at least $300(and purchase for $200) in order to meet my $100threshold. Depending on your threshold and average profit margins, your targets and goals may be different from mine.

Speaking of which, you are free to set your own target profit threshold wherever you would like. However, please, please, please do not sell yourself short. You might be thinking, "Steve has a $100 threshold and an average profit margin of 34%... but maybe I could 'start' by aiming to make $10 per sale at a 10% profit margin..."

No.

This is exactly the type of mindset that does not work. It is a defensive, protective frame of mind that is really saying, "I do not think I can do this, so I am going to aim low to maximize my limited chances of success."

It is much more powerful and effective to take an offensive mindset, realizing that, with a high goal in mind, you are much more likely to achieve it. Set a threshold and stick to it. Then aim for that threshold or better in all your deals. I recommend at least $50-100 for practical purposes.

Realize that you might only do a handful of transactions in a month, so if you maintain your threshold at this level, then you stand to make a decent chunk of change on a revolving basis. You probably will not get rich making a mere $100-200 per month, but at least you will be able to monetize your hobby, rather than having it be another expense on your budget. Hey, a couple hundred bucks is a couple hundred bucks.

On the other hand, if you lower your threshold to, say, $25, or worse, $10, you decrease profitability and open yourself up to a lot more risk. Not only will you be barely making anything for your efforts, but the risk that you might lose money on a sale becomes greater.

For instance, say you have predicted that you will make at least $75.00 on a particular deal. If it turns out your market value estimate is wrong by $25.00, then you will only end up netting $50.00 on the deal. On the other hand, if you started out only aiming to make $25.00, then you will break even or worse when you discover your market value estimate was wrong.

Therefore, you can think of my "$100 threshold" not only as a goal in itself but as a buffer against loss. For those products you just cannot seem to sell for a long time (after three months, for example), you have more room to move the price down without going into the red.

Cash Management, Accounting, and Related Financial Metrics

Speaking of thresholds, let's talk about Cash Management for a minute.

Cash Management... ugh. Isn't that, like, Accounting?

Let's get something straight. If you have the luxury of cash to manage, you should be happy to keep track of it in a halfway sensible manner! This counts both in terms of managing your actual, physical cash and accounting for your sales history over time. Being sloppy with cash and accounting is simply unacceptable, and will hinder your ability to track your progress.

Physical Handling of Cash

This is the first, most direct part of cash management. As in, you have some cash in your wallet right this very moment... now what do you *do* with it?

Earlier on, in Chapter 2, we discussed the importance of maintaining separate mental "compartments" for your personal life and your business. The way you must implement this in real life is by maintaining two completely separate physical stacks of cash.

For example, my wallet actually has two separate cash compartments. One I use for my personal cash, and the other I use for my Craigslist cash. Occasionally I will "borrow" a $20 bill from one compartment and return it later on, but I try to avoid this for the sake of keeping things straight. You want to remove the temptation to inject the cash you are making with your side business into your personal life.

In your personal life, you *spend* money on things that generally do not provide a return. Whether you are buying food, entertainment, or anything else, odds are that the money is gone forever after the purchase.

On the other hand, what we are learning about in this book is how to *invest* money into inventory and sell it at a profit. Your dollars are therefore much more valuable in the "business" compartment of your wallet, because as long as they stay there, you have more available funds to invest into your inventory, which in turns becomes more cash.

Note that in your personal life, you do not change the way you look at cash. You still pay your bills, feel the pain when you spend too much on a Friday night, and feel guilty when your girlfriend/wife or boyfriend/husband finds out you bought something you did not need. I'm talking about the kind of guilt that comes with spending that extra $4.25 you shouldn't have spent on a latte.

With your business, though, it is a different ball game. You have separate money set aside for this compartment of your life and nobody has the right to complain about how you use it. You do not feel guilty when you spend business funds, and you do not need to, because the business is its own independent entity.

Once you get the hang of it, this business compartment might even feel fictional, like a video game. You might come to view your business cash more like game credits, which is a powerful frame of mind to be in. Whether you use these "game credits" to buy yourself a $4.25 latte or an $800 inventory item, the only emotions present are ones of opportunity and advancement.

Now, depending on your personal goals, you may at some point wish to spend some of the cash you have earned on things that do not provide a return. After all, it is nice to treat yourself here and there after building up sufficient cash to do so.

However, if you do treat yourself, be sure such purchases do not significantly affect your supply of available cash. Note that I would never wipe out my cash supply entirely with careless spending. I always make sure to have at least a few hundred dollars on hand, if not more, to snatch up a good deal when it comes up (and as a general insight, I also try to maintain at least $1,500 or more in inventory at any given time, if not closer to $4,000-5,000). The last thing you want is to see a fantastic deal surface, then realize you are unable to capitalize on it because you do not have cash available to complete the purchase.

Remember, maintaining your purchasing power keeps the flame lit.

This is how you "stay in the game" and continue generating more deals and cash well into the future, which is the goal. This, in turn, allows you to grow your inventory, increase your cash supply, treat yourself more often, and potentially inject money into other business ventures.

Again, the more you reinvest your earnings back into the business, the quicker you can scale the business and grow your cash supply. You can literally see this happening when you look at my sales data in Appendix A. I started off pretty slow, with some small-time deals in the beginning, but once I gained momentum, my growing cash supply allowed for an increase in inventory, sales, and you guessed it – profit.

If at any point, I had blown all that cash on something for immediate gratification in my personal life, the gears would have ground to a halt, and my forward progress would have slowed to a crawl as I struggled to get started back up again. Instead, I kept the momentum moving in the right direction and am *still* leveraging that momentum today.

Therefore, try not to look at Craigslist as a means of achieving a simple end. For instance, do not fall into the trap of *"Once I make $1,000, I'm going to buy that guitar I wanted and be done."* While I suppose you could use these skills in that manner, I would strongly encourage you to wait until you make, say, $2,000, then buy your guitar, and still have $1,000 to keep things rolling. This requires some self-discipline, but it pays off in the end.

There is one more thing I would like to share on the subject of cash, while we're on it: use cash as a powerful motivator. Whether you keep your business cash in your wallet or somewhere else, take a moment every now and again to appreciate the liquidity of your currency and the things it can bring you. It may sound silly, but taking a few bills out and holding them in your hand for a minute can actually be quite therapeutic.

In modern society, many people avoid showing appreciation for their earnings because they wish to avoid being seen as greedy. Yet it is healthy to reflect upon and appreciate the things we have, especially those things that we have truly worked for and earned, and recognize our efforts in a positive manner. There is a difference between privately appreciating and publicly gloating, after all.

Through this private appreciation of your accomplishments, you can positively reinforce the habits and behaviors that led you there in the first place. This creates a positive feedback loop that fuels an upward spiral of growth, achievement, and further appreciation.

Keeping the Books

Now we will explore the other side of cash management, which has more to do with financial accounting and using some additional metrics to analyze your business over time. First, it is important to understand how you benefit from good accounting practices.

As soon as you start recording your purchases and sales, you will gain extra *motivation* from seeing the numbers. You will calculate totals, figure out profit margin percentages, and track your progress, all of which can help give you energy and motivation to reach the next level.

Without any sort of accounting system, you are flying blind. You might not know when you are having a slow month, nor will you be able to fully appreciate a really strong month. There is less opportunity for reflection, and a decreased ability to measure and analyze results.

Sales managers around the world know how important it is to keep an eye on the numbers. It keeps a fire lit underneath our butts that drives us forward to the next deal. This does not mean numbers are the end-all, be-all of sales, but they are clearly important.

Heck, I would not have been able to write this book without proper accounts of all my transactions. I probably would have forgotten about some of them altogether, forgotten the amounts I bought/sold certain things for, and would not have been able to accurately convey my experiences to you, my reader.

I strongly encourage you to start a spreadsheet and keep track of your purchases and sales. I use the spreadsheet feature in Google Docs to do it and it is super easy. I can be on any computer, my phone, a tablet, or another device, and make quick updates anytime I buy or sell.

Appendix A contains an abridged table of my own sales information, copied from my personal records for you to examine. Due to space constraints, though, I have eliminated certain fields. Here are the basic data fields I would recommend you include:

Date Acquired | Date Sold | Type | Item | Paid | Sold | Margin

1. Date Acquired
This is the date you acquire or purchase a new item.

2. Date Sold
This is the date you sell an item.

3. Type
This field contains several possible values: *For Sale, Gain, Loss, Hard Cost, Keep.* This is essentially a status field that helps you classify each line item, which comes in handy when using the sort feature to organize your spreadsheet.

For Sale is used to mark current, unsold inventory.
Gain and *Loss* are used to classify sold items.
Hard Cost is for tracking any expenses incurred.

Keep is used to identify items you intend to hold onto for a while, or keep for personal use rather than to resell.

I also use a field called *Pos CF*, short for "positive cash flow," to denote new cash injected into my fund pool by the sale of *existing items* that I already own. In other words, with these items, I am not accounting for the original purchase price, which might have been years ago – I am simply recording the additional cash generated by the sale for fundraising purposes.

4. Item
This is the name, make, and/or model of the item in question.

5. Paid
This is where you will list what you paid for an item.

6. Sold
This is where you will list the amount you sold the item for.

7. Margin
This is a calculation of your profit margin. The formula you will use for this in MS Excel is = (Sold -Paid)/Sold. You should format this column to read as a percentage.

***

Once you have some sales history, you can get fancy if you'd like by calculating Average Profit per Transaction, Net Profit Margin, Return on Time (ROT), and Return on Investment (ROI). These are additional metrics that I cover in Appendix B, and while they are not crucial to your success, they are valuable to understand the state of your business.

To make this process easier for you, I have created a shared Google Docs spreadsheet that automatically calculates all of these metrics for you – both on an individual sale basis and a collective, total basis. For each item you buy and resell, all you have to do is plug in the purchase price and sale price, and the spreadsheet does the rest! Here is the link:

http://bit.ly/1vvn6er

Use this template to jump-start your success, or create your own version if you'd like —either way, be sure to track your purchase and sales data from the very beginning. This will keep you organized and on track from the outset, and keep you from needing to go back at some point and fill in blanks.

Conclusion

To run an effective business of any scale, it is important to set financial boundaries, properly manage your physical cash, and account for your progress over time.

On a day-to-day basis, the most important consideration is simply ensuring that you hit an established profit threshold. In the long run, tracking your sales data can provide extra motivation and the opportunity to reflect on your activities. Finally, knowing how to calculate additional metrics like Net Profit Margin, ROT, and ROI can help you analyze your business from additional angles, providing extra information to ensure you are most effectively investing your time and money.

CHAPTER 5 RECAP

- Set a *profit threshold* to be sure a given deal is worth your time. I recommend a minimum target of $50-100.
- Properly manage your physical cash, ideally in a separate compartment from the cash used for your personal expenses.
- Begin using a spreadsheet (you can use my template free of charge) to track your financials from Day 1.
- Optionally, familiarize yourself with Appendix B to gain a greater handle on your financials as you progress.

Use this chapter as a reminder to set high goals for yourself and not to settle for paltry sums. Specifically, set a profit threshold and stick to it; then be confident in your ability to create deals around that number. Maintaining this positive, action-oriented agenda is what will separate you from the crowd. It will also help you stay emotionally resilient and financially stable through the occasional misstep, as you will write off bad deals quickly.

Assignments

1. Set a profit threshold that makes sense for your niche, but be sure that your target threshold is in the neighborhood of at least $50-100. Aside from the fact that you want to maximize your gains, aiming lower than this will open you up to additional and unnecessary risk.

2. Create your spreadsheet in Google Docs and start using it to keep track of your sales data.

On Deck

In the next chapter, we will explore the core fundamentals you must learn to properly analyze deals. Namely, we will review the proper frame of mind for approaching any transaction, the key economic principles at play, and the specific methods I use to calculate and determine buy/sell prices for any given item.

6

SELL LOW, BUY LOWER

THE POWER OF INTELLIGENT DATA ANALYSIS

In this chapter, we will review an essential component of transacting profitable business on Craigslist: properly analyzing market data to determine the correct prices at which to buy and sell. In any financial market, this is truly the name of the game, and Craigslist is no exception.

Preparation
Planning & Measuring
Deal Analysis
Purchasing
Sales

Focus on Selling Competitively

Throughout the entire process of analyzing prices and evaluating individual deals, my mind stays focused like a laser beam on one thing: the eventual sale. More specifically, the *price* attached to that future sale. *"What can I sell this item for?"* is a question that continues to echo throughout my mind from the moment I commence analysis to the moment an item is sold.

Answering this one question makes my life very simple, after all. Once I know what an item will sell for, I know what price it must be purchased for to meet or exceed my profit threshold. This in turn allows me to be more efficient in deciding which listings are worthwhile to make offers on and which are not, and the exact amounts to offer on those listings.

Of course, there is always room for play and negotiation on the actual front of communications (for example, offering a little less than you would actually be willing to pay, with the idea of increasing your offer if you encounter resistance; similarly, it is advisable to publish a higher listed price when posting an item for sale than you would actually be willing to accept). However, the idea stands that once you identify your target sales price, or perhaps more accurately the minimum that you want to get out of the sale, the analysis phase ends and the purchasing process commences. You easily move from "What can I sell this for?" to "Who will I buy this from?"

We need to adopt a sales-driven frame of mind, then, in order to properly approach preliminary analysis and purchasing. Finding that initial sales price target gives us the ability to calculate a good purchase price and get to work finding that deal.

One way to get into this powerful, sales-focused frame of mind is to consider your existing paradigm for sales and evaluate its usefulness.

Now, I'm not sure exactly what your background is with regards to sales, so I'm not going to make any assumptions. However, regardless of your background or experience, or lack thereof, all of us have surely heard the phrase, *Buy Low, Sell High*. Even if you are not familiar with the stock market, you have probably come across this phrase at one point or another. It makes sense, because selling higher than you buy means you will earn a profit.

"Buy Low, Sell High" is indiscriminate, to my mind, though—all it tells us is that we need to buy and sell at arbitrary prices that are necessarily different. When you really think about it, this is useless information, since it is obvious that you must sell higher than you buy to stay in business.

Now call me a cork sniffing hair-splitter, but I believe there is a shift in perspective that happens when you rephrase this to *"Sell Low, Buy Lower."*

Can you spot the paradigm shift?

"Sell Low, Buy Lower" makes an important distinction on the sales side. It brings the primary focus to the sale, and you are no longer selling "high."Instead, you are selling at "low," *competitive market prices.* Prices you know you can sell at, because they are acceptable from a buyer's perspective.

You see, when you rely on selling "high," (higher than the competitive average, so to speak) you limit yourself to a smaller audience of buyers who are able and willing to pay a higher amount. Your profit margin also shrinks, even at the same level of net profit, due to simple mathematics. (To understand the math behind this shrinking profit margin phenomenon, please refer to Appendix C.)

In contrast, by selling "low," you open yourself to a much larger pool of buyers, who are eager to pay a competitive price to win the item. This means more buyer inquiries, more offers, and faster turnover. In turn, this yields higher velocity of cash, better profit margins, and accelerated compounding of profits.

Note that selling competitively implies you will also be *buying* at very low prices. After all, you still need to put a markup on your purchased goods before turning around and selling them at a competitive price, and this is only possible if you can find great deals on the purchasing side. Finding these deals may seem like a chore at times, but it is not by any means insurmountable. Plus, look on the bright side: every time you make an acquisition, your sales forecast is already looking pretty good.

The big question, then, is how exactly *do* we figure out the competitive sale price for any given item?

Economic Equilibrium is "Competitive"

In order to define "competitive" in terms of dollars and cents, we will need a primer on the basic economic concept of supply and demand.

The graphs that follow might make this concept seem a little "technical," but I promise you it is quite simple and intuitive. If for any reason you find yourself getting lost in the graphs, just remember that consumers tend to demand a higher quantity of a product when the price is lower, and conversely, they demand a lower quantity of a product when its price is higher.

A Primer on Supply & Demand

Here is a graph every econ student knows all too well:

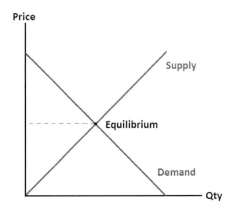

Econ 101 - The Forces of Supply & Demand

Definitions
The Y axis ("**P**") is Price.
The X axis ("**Qty**") is Quantity.

Quantity supplied is the amount suppliers plan to sell in a certain time period at a particular price. This amount can be determined by referencing the **supply** curve.

Quantity demanded is the amount consumers plan to purchase in a certain time period at a particular price. This amount can be determined by referencing the **demand** curve.

Equilibrium occurs at a point where the supply and demand curves intersect, and represents a price and quantity that satisfies the interests of both buyers and sellers in a market in a given time period. Notably, it is at or near this equilibrium point that we consider prices to be competitive – and this is approximately where we should aim to resell our inventory.

Analysis

Understand that the supply and demand curves represent market forces that drive sales and purchasing in the collective market. At any point in time, if the price increases, buyers will demand a lower quantity of a given product. Conversely, price increases trigger sellers to supply a higher quantity of a given product to capture the additional profit at stake.

Here is an example of what happens to quantity demanded when prices increase:

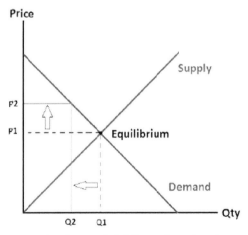

Quantity demanded falls as the price rises

When our initial price P1 moves away from equilibrium and increases to the higher price P2, the quantity demanded falls from Q1 to Q2.

Notice how this change in quantity demanded is different from a *change in demand* itself. The following graph shows what a decrease in demand itself will look like. Notice how the actual demand curve shifts from D1 to D2.

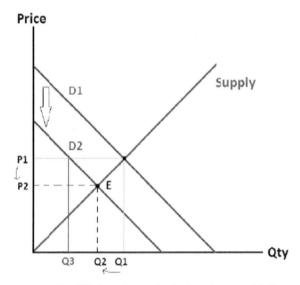

A new Equilibrium is reached when Demand falls

When demand itself drops, it means buyers will purchase a lesser quantity at the same price point, and a new equilibrium is reached. Specifically, when the demand curve shifts from D1 to D2, the quantity demanded for price P1 changes from Q1 to Q3. Moreover, a new equilibrium point is reached at (Q2, P2).

Without graphing every possible scenario, you can imagine how an *increase* in demand would push D1 up and outward, raising the equilibrium price.

Similarly, you can visualize how an *increase* in supply would push the supply curve out to the right and down (lowering the equilibrium price), whereas a *decrease* in supply would push the supply curve in to the left and up (raising the equilibrium price).

Key Takeaways

We could go into more detail, but that would be beyond the scope of this book. Those interested in pursuing this subject further should read *Principles of Economics* by Robert Frank and Ben Bernanke, which I would recommend, or any of the many additional books and resources available on the subject of Microeconomics. For now, let's simply review what we can take away from this mini-lesson.

First, the biggest take away from this lesson is that *the equilibrium price is the target price we want to sell at or near*. This is because it is the "competitive" point, where buyers and sellers tend to agree on an item's valuation.

Branching off of this is the fact that *the equilibrium price will almost always tend to hover a bit below the average of listed asking prices*. We did not actually discuss this inference in the last section, but I am telling it to you now, and we will dive further into this in the next section.

Next, it is valuable to understand supply and demand from a big picture perspective as a general matter, because understanding these market forces will help you draw stronger insights from patterns observed in the sales listings on Craigslist.

For instance, perhaps you notice an item listed several times at or near $700, but months and months go by and those listings are still there —clearly those items have not sold. Despite what the asking price data suggests, then, we can safely assume that the true equilibrium price is lower. The sellers aren't getting any traction with buyers because the quantity demanded at $700 is not very high.

Likewise, maybe you commonly see another item listed around $500, but those listings tend to disappear within days or even hours of being posted. One might assume the $500 price point is fairly close to the true equilibrium price in that case, since buyers are clearly jumping at those opportunities.

As a third takeaway from our mini lesson, understanding supply and demand will help you stay sharp as things change in your niche's surrounding market. Instead of using current and historical price data as a sole predictor of an item's equilibrium price, you can strengthen the results and conclusions you might draw from this data by incorporating additional information.

As an example, we have already seen how I bought and sold a number of Epiphone Les Paul Standard guitars – all right around the same buy/sell prices. The fact that I have repeated this process so many times, and nearly always at the same prices, gives me great confidence in my estimation of the correct prices at which to buy and sell this item in the future.

However, what if Epiphone (the manufacturer) makes an announcement that they will be permanently discontinuing the Les Paul model? Well, the principle of scarcity tells us something is more valuable when there is less of it available, and true to form, most hobbyists do find some additional value in owning an item that "you can't even buy new!" This would lead to an increase in demand, however marginal, and a higher equilibrium price would result. If I was currently sitting on inventory of this item, it might be prudent of me to raise my asking price. If I was not currently sitting on any inventory of this item, it might be time to snatch up whatever is available at the existing equilibrium before "word gets out" and things change.

On the other hand, what if it leaks that Epiphone employs child labor in abusive sweatshops in the manufacturing of this particular model? The outrage over such business practices would lead to a decrease in demand, and a lower equilibrium price would result.

Similarly, say a key influencer (in this case, perhaps a well-respected and followed guitar player) makes a statement that he or she would "never play an Epiphone Les Paul" for whatever reason, erroneous or not. This can also lead to a decrease in demand, since the influencer's audience (and our potential buyers) might now perceive this item to be less desirable. "I would have paid $300 for that guitar yesterday, dude, but now they just aren't as cool anymore..."

In addition to the above examples of factors that may shift demand in a market, here are some additional factors that may cause such a shift in either direction.

Additional Factors that Influence Demand

- *Consumer Preferences* (discussed above)
  These might be statements from an industry influencer or leader, news reports that reveal good or bad ethics of a product manufacturer, or "fad" trends that everyone seems to be following.

- *Number of Consumers*
  Generally speaking, as the population of buyers increases within a market, demand will increase and drive prices up. For instance, in a town where more people skateboard than on average, the price for used skateboards will likely be higher than in towns where fewer people take up the hobby. (Tip: in such a situation, you might buy used skateboards in the next town over where demand, and therefore price, is lower; then move them across markets into the town where demand, and therefore price, is higher. Of course, the existence of increased Supply in this town could drive the price down, negating the price effects of the increased Demand.)

- *Buying Power*
  If the economy is strong and growing, and your buyers have increasing personal income, expect demand to increase. On the other hand, when a recession hits and people are losing

jobs, demand falls – especially for luxury items or "extras" that are not basic living expenses.

- *Future Expectations*
  This could be anything that affects a buyer's perception of future events, such as a news report indicating a product will be discontinued (discussed above), or a prediction that prices will rise or fall.

- *Prices of Related Goods*
  Normally, when we talk about related goods, we automatically think of **substitutes** – a similar product made by a different manufacturer, for example. If the price of a substitute decreases, people buy more of the substitute and demand for the original product decreases. As an example, it can be annoying when you are selling a product and someone lists the same thing for much less – you can understand how this hurts your ability to sell.

  In addition to substitutes, the price of **complements** also affects demand. Complements are products that go hand in hand with one another, such as guitars and guitar strings, hamburgers and hamburger buns, music and iPods, and so on. When the price of a complement increases, demand for the original product decreases. For example, if the average price of guitars goes up, fewer guitars will be purchased and, as a result, fewer guitar strings will be purchased.

It is noteworthy that there are factors that cause shifts in supply, too, but for our purposes, it is sufficient to focus on those factors that primarily deal cause a change in demand.

As we move into the following sections, keep these demand-altering factors in the back of your mind and consider how they might affect your estimation of equilibrium. There is no need to get carried away performing mass research to account for all of these factors, but it is good to have an understanding of them, so you can make connections as you naturally stumble upon new information in the course of your daily life.

Estimating the Equilibrium Point

In the prior section, we discussed how the equilibrium price is a general target for our eventual sale price. Note that this does not mean we will not *list* our product for sale at a higher price; rather, it is more like the "target minimum" we expect to get.

We also talked about some things that might influence demand for a given product, effectively adjusting our current or future estimation of equilibrium. These are more complex factors that frankly you do not need to worry about *too* much, but which can be helpful when you become knowledgeable in your niche.

Before we "adjust" our estimation of equilibrium, though, how do we truly estimate equilibrium to begin with?

In the absence of personal transaction history, *current and historical asking-price data* is what I use more than anything else to make predictions about the equilibrium price for an item. By roughly calculating the average of these asking prices – sometimes over time, sometimes in a single data-gathering session – and applying a downward adjustment to this average, I arrive at my equilibrium price estimate.

What I am really trying to figure out through this process is the actual *average sale price*. I know there is some relationship between the average asking price and the actual average sale price for any given item, and my goal is to utilize my knowledge of that relationship to predict things I do not know from the things I do know.

The "relationship" between these two averages is simple enough; since sellers on Craigslist tend to get a little less during the actual sale than they ask for – due to the nature of Craigslist, where people often haggle and bargain—we can conclude that actual average sale prices will be a bit lower than the average asking prices visible in the listings.

This is the key guiding question to ask, then: *What are other sellers listing it for?*

Of course, more useful to know would be what sellers are *actually* "selling it for," since recent sales comparables would be the ideal data to have for analysis. (Sales comps are largely how real estate appraisers and agents estimate home values, for example.)However, since it would be impractical to go about collecting such data, we do the next best thing and approximate it by applying our best-guess adjustment factor to the average of asking prices.

By aggregating data points from actual sales listings, you can begin coming up with an idea of how pricing works for a particular product in your market, and begin to figure out the average asking price.

The more data points, the better, so check Craigslist, eBay, retailer sites with used sections, web forums, and any other market with accessible data. Performing a quick Google search for an item is a great way to find such alternative markets. You can even browse Craigslist in other cities and states if you would like to collect further price information, although your home city will always be the most directly relevant, assuming you are selling in your home city.

Obtaining cold hard data like this is king and minimizes guesswork. The more data you have, the more your confidence will increase that you understand the product you are dealing with, its pricing, and the market for it. This gives you more than enough information to figure out a decent equilibrium estimate.

This process does not need to take all that much time, either. In the beginning, it may take you longer as you seek to learn your niche and its products (we originally discussed this in Chapter 4 with regards to general product research and familiarization). But even then, it still doesn't take long to type the name of your item into a search bar and pull up some quick results in Craigslist and eBay. After a few minutes of browsing, you will probably have most of the information you need.

Remember, all we're talking about doing here is glancing over a handful of numbers or so and roughly averaging them, then subtracting off a small bit for good measure. To put it in context, this is plain old arithmetic – albeit with a little judgment involved for figuring out the final subtraction to estimate the true difference between the average asking prices and actual average sale prices, or true equilibrium.

Note that putting in a bunch of time here does not equate to superior results, either, and may actually harm your return on time (and morale). In fact, despite what this chapter might suggest, you should spend relatively little time aggregating data points to keep the whole process efficient. Keep that in mind as we move along with this chapter.

Moving forward, we will look at the specific methods I use to gather data from Craigslist, eBay, Retailers with used sections, and Web Forums. As you read through these methods, remember that the most relevant data is that which you find on Craigslist. Other markets like eBay can provide great supplemental information, but what you really want to focus on is the data you can collect on Craigslist itself.

Data Collection on Craigslist

When I start looking at products I have not purchased before, data collection *on Craigslist* is the first thing I do. I might even scan data points in other cities/markets on Craigslist (in addition to my own) to see where sellers are pricing the product. For instance, when I am looking at pricing for an Epiphone Les Paul Standard, I might type those very words into the Craigslist search bar and see what comes up. Then, I can begin constructing my average from the prices shown.

Below are sample results for this very search from January 2014. By the way, you might notice that these search results are a little more "focused" and specific than the similar results we saw in Chapter 4 (in that chapter, we only searched for the words "Les Paul," whereas here we are searching for "Epiphone Les Paul Standard").

In this particular search, I only circled the prices that I felt were relevant. The reason I put a thin box around the guitar listed as a "pro" model is because that may be a completely different item, and I do not want to compare apples and oranges.

This is important to pay attention to. You need to make sure you do not factor price information into your averages from products that *seem* similar, but which are in fact *completely different* from the product in question. This is the same principle we originally highlighted two chapters ago when discussing the differences between seemingly similar automobiles, such as Ford's base V6 model Mustang versus their more expensive GT, V8 model Mustang.

Common differences you should look out for when researching your niche's products include brand, make, model, production year, production location, size, and any other specific features can turn something into an "orange" quickly – such as anything with the words "sport," "premium," "limited edition," and so on.

Remember also that an item's condition can affect price, and therefore is useful to factor in alongside these other considerations when calculating your price averages. Ask yourself: is a given item in great shape, or does it show significant wear and tear? We can all appreciate how items in poor condition do not warrant the same asking price as similar items in excellent condition.

To make things even more interesting, you might ask yourself if a given product in the listings is actually an "orange," or just an "apple of a different color."

In the case of the "pro" model guitar listed in the search results above, this is truly an in-between situation, but it is more like an orange than an apple. From niche experience, I know it has different electronics and technology built into it than the others, and therefore its price should not be directly compared to the product in question.

The left-handed guitar, though, is still an "apple," despite its variation in orientation (this is more like an "apple of a different color"), and so are the other guitars that are literally different colors but still the same instrument. They have the same wood, same design, and same electronics and technology – and therefore they can be directly compared when evaluating pricing, despite a different paint job. *Capice?*

Before finalizing my equilibrium price in this example, something else I noticed in these listings is that all of the guitars come with hard cases, *except* for the left-handed one – and this explains why it is priced a bit lower than the rest. If it included a hard case, instead of being priced at $325, it would probably be around the $375-400mark like the other listings. Therefore, when calculating my average price across these instruments, I should probably substitute an adjusted value of $375-400 for this particular left-handed guitar for a more relevant comparison.

Now at this point, with all these little factors accounted for, you might be tempted to take the simple average of asking prices to come up with your equilibrium price estimate. That's not quite right, though. Remember, most sellers on Craigslist eventually sell their items for less than their listed asking prices (due to negotiation), so we need to make an adjustment.

In this particular case, I would arrive at an equilibrium estimate of $325-350,based on my feeling that these prices are somewhere in the neighborhood of $25-75 too high – call it a $50 adjustment for the sake of simplicity. Perhaps it would be conservative of me to set my target sales price around $325, though, so when I actually create my sales listing, I might list around $360-370 and hope to negotiate to $350 with an interested buyer.

Now, you might be wondering what gave me the "feeling" that these prices needed to be adjusted by about $50 to estimate true equilibrium.

Figuring out the proper adjustment will largely be based on judgment and experience; the ultimate form of experience is past purchasing/sales data for a given item, since you will have a good idea of the functional price range (high/low points the item can be bought and resold at). That being said, below I have listed some very general guidelines that you can use as a starting point when analyzing data on Craigslist in particular.

If the current/historical "average" of asking prices is less than or equal to $200, the "adjustment" needed to estimate true equilibrium is probably near $20-30.

If the current/historical "average" of asking prices is between $200 and $500, the "adjustment" needed to estimate true equilibrium is probably near $30-50.

If the current/historical "average" of asking prices is between $500 and $1,250, the "adjustment" needed to estimate true equilibrium is probably near $50-150.

If the current/historical "average" of asking prices is between$1,250 and $2,000, the "adjustment" needed to estimate true equilibrium is probably near$150-200.

You'll notice in all these cases that my suggested "adjustment" is around 85-95% of the "average" of asking prices. The exact percentages *will* vary depending on item and niche, but this should at least put you in the ballpark when you start out.

Leveraging eBay for Additional Price Information

Let's talk about active eBay listings for a minute, since they can be such a good source of information to supplement what you find on Craigslist. In fact, I have sometimes relied entirely on eBay's price information to justify a new purchase.

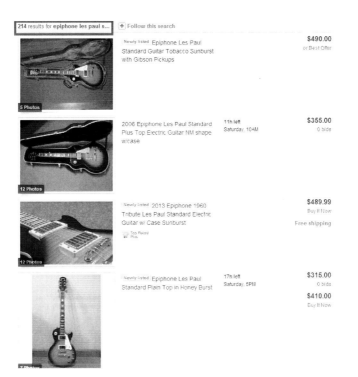

Here again, we are searching for "Epiphone Les Paul Standard," and eBay's pricing looks even higher than what we saw on Craigslist, which further validates that our previously-calculated equilibrium price is "safe." However, when looking at eBay prices, remember that you are really looking at two different prices: the price listed (which is what you would pay as a buyer), and 86% of the listed price (which is how much you would get as the seller, because 14% disappears between eBay's final value fee and PayPal's transaction fee).

In fact, each of these prices is relevant in its own way, but since we are focusing on coming up with an equilibrium estimate for our target *sales* price, we should focus on the price received after the fees are removed. Thus, even though we see prices hovering around $400, multiplying 0.86 * $400 = $344, which is much closer to our previous equilibrium estimation of $325-350.

Something you may be wondering about is the potential cost of *shipping* on eBay, and how that might affect our estimate of Equilibrium. One of the above listings advertises free shipping, but the others do not – and shipping does represent an additional cost to the *buyer* in those cases. In the case of free shipping, it represents an additional cost to the *seller*.

Generally speaking, I would not worry too much about shipping fees when calculating your equilibrium price for Craigslist. Trying to estimate the exact amount of shipping a buyer will pay on eBay is tough, since it will depend on their geographic location. Who knows if the eventual buyer resides in the same state as the seller, where shipping costs will be lower, or if they are on the other end of the universe, where shipping costs will be higher. Still, for certain types of items that do necessitate expensive shipping methods, it can be helpful to keep in mind that shipping costs can have an effect on the transaction.

For example, if we see that a buyer has paid $375 for an item, plus an estimated $40 in shipping, we might be able to deduce that there

are similar local buyers willing to pay a total of $415 for that item –
and as a local seller without the need to ship, perhaps you can
capture that additional $40 as profit instead of funneling it into a
hard cost for shipping. Not to mention the fact that you won't be
giving away 14% of your sale to eBay and PayPal.

On the other hand, many buyers on eBay do accept shipping as a
"cost of doing business" and might not be inclined to pay the
additional amount when transacting locally on Craigslist, especially
since people expect to negotiate more and perhaps get better prices
through a medium like Craigslist. Hence, shipping is truly a wishy-
washy "metric" to measure, but on a case-by-case basis, may provide
us with some useful information to take into account as a correlating
factor alongside our existing data analysis.

By the way, pointing out the extra cost of shipping on eBay can be a
powerful argument when negotiating on Craigslist, not to mention
the fact that on eBay you cannot try before you buy."Sure, you found
my item for $20 less on eBay, but after you pay $30 for shipping, it
will actually be more expensive, and you won't have an opportunity
to verify its condition before making a non-refundable purchase."

Another powerful secret to price analysis on eBay is to search the
sold listings via eBay's advanced search:

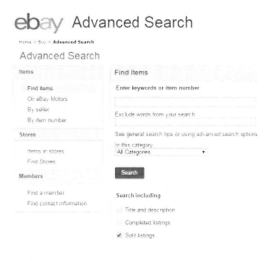

To access these listings, simply go to the following link: http://www.ebay.com/sch/ebayadvsearch/

Then type in the name of your product, select the "Sold Listings" checkbox, and click Search. You may also want to scroll down a bit and check the box for "Used" to avoid getting new products mixed in with the search results.

This will give you actual historical data on sold items, in most cases showing the actual price those items sold for unless there was a "best offer" accepted. Browsing through these listings, you will want to keep in mind some of the same things we discussed in the previous section regarding comparing apples and oranges, etc. The nice thing is that this can be a quick way to skim through literally hundreds of actual sold listings.

Retailers with Used Sections

As yet another way to aggregate additional data for your analysis on an item, you may wish to seek out retailers that have a relevant "used section" on their website. For example, in my case, the very popular Guitar Center has a site devoted to this purpose: to display used items available for sale at their many locations. (See: http://used.guitarcenter.com/)

If we do a quick search for Epiphone Les Paul guitars on their site, this is what we see:

No Image Available	⊛ JUST ARRIVED ⊛ SOLIDBODY ELECTRIC Les Paul Standard Used Epiphone Les Paul Standard Heritage Cherry Su	Guitars	Guitar Center Southcenter Tukwila, Washington 98188 206-243-9077 View Store's Used Inventory	Now Only $349.99
110544017	☆☆☆ Details »		Contact Store	
	⊛ JUST ARRIVED ⊛ SOLIDBODY ELECTRIC Les Paul Standard Used Epiphone Les Paul Standard Honey Burst Solid	Guitars	Guitar Center Gwinnett Lawrenceville, Georgia 30044 678-380-6730 View Store's Used Inventory	Now Only $349.99
110638968	☆☆☆ Details »		Contact Store	
No Image Available	⊛ JUST ARRIVED ⊛ SOLIDBODY ELECTRIC Les Paul Standard Used Epiphone Les Paul Standard Solid Body Electri	Guitars	Guitar Center New Orleans Harahan, Louisiana 70123 504-818-0336 View Store's Used Inventory	Now Only $299.99
110545419	☆☆☆ Details »		Contact Store	
No Image Available	⊛ JUST ARRIVED ⊛ SOLIDBODY ELECTRIC Les Paul Standard Used Epiphone Les Paul Standard Tobacco Sunburst S	Guitars	Guitar Center Little Rock Little Rock, Arkansas 72211 501-225-3700 View Store's Used Inventory	Now Only $299.99
110633833	☆☆☆☆ Details »		Contact Store	
No Image Available	SOLIDBODY ELECTRIC Les Paul Standard Used Epiphone Les Paul Standard Solid Body Electri	Guitars	Guitar Center Lakeland Lakeland, Florida 33805 863-665-4590 View Store's Used Inventory	Now Only $324.99
110490898	☆☆☆ Details »		Contact Store	
	SOLIDBODY ELECTRIC Les Paul Standard Used Epiphone Les Paul Standard Solid Body Electri	Guitars	Guitar Center Ocean Ocean, New Jersey 07712 732-493-0614 View Store's Used Inventory	Now Only $349.99
110547561	☆☆☆ Details »		Contact Store	

Like with eBay, these listings might be best taken with a grain of salt, because shipping could be a factor if the buyer does not live in the town where the item is being sold. Plus, there will naturally be differences in income level and other factors, and thus demand, from one city to another. However, once again we have the benefit of seeing quite a few additional data points that might help strengthen our overall analysis. In this case, what I am seeing here continues to validate my equilibrium estimate of $325-350.

Web Forums and other markets

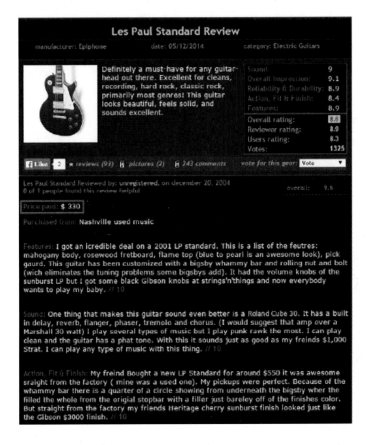

In any niche, you will need to do your own online research to determine where groups of people "hang out" and discuss products of a certain type. In my niche, one example of such a place is the product review forum at http://www.ultimate-guitar.com/

In the screenshot above, you can see one such review posted for my trusty Epiphone Les Paul Standard. Importantly, most of the users who post reviews on this site will also tell you the price they paid. In this case, we can see that this particular user paid $330 for his guitar from a used music shop in Nashville, once again seeming to validate our estimate of Equilibrium.

However, I should point out that if you skim through all of the reviews on this page (there are 93 total at http://www.ultimate-guitar.com/reviews/electric_guitars/epiphone/les_paul_standard), you will see a variety of price points. This is because many folks are posting prices that they paid for the item *brand new*, while others bought theirs used. Therefore, we must be careful to decipher what is really happening with the data, so as to not compare apples and oranges. Notice also that on such review pages, reviews that are more recent should carry more weight than those that are quite old, and perhaps irrelevant.

Of course, even with the need to decipher all of this, it is still nice to have the additional data points to reference. Plus, in the case of web forums, you may even learn some useful information about the products you are buying and selling – including certain points that could come into play during price negotiations. Any extra knowledge you can acquire about your products and niche will make you a smarter buyer and more capable seller.

Tracking Data Over Time

This is what my "graph" might look like over the course of many weeks as I track an item's asking price. These data points would normally be composed primarily of Craigslist asking price data points, but may also incorporate some from the other marketplaces we reviewed (eBay, Retailers' sites, Web Forums).

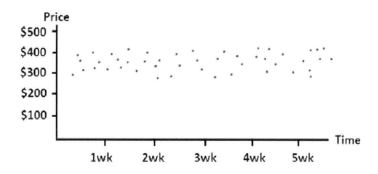

With all this data, I can more easily intuit the item's average asking price (the purpose of collecting the data to begin with):

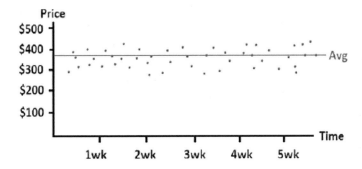

Then finally, I will apply an adjustment factor (I provided some loose guidelines for this earlier in the chapter) to estimate my true equilibrium price:

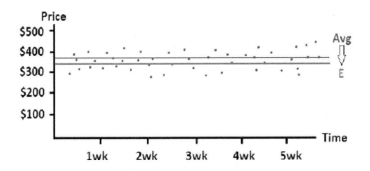

Note that you do not necessarily need to track an item's asking price data over time in order to come up with an average. If you are working with a new item you have never researched before, you can apply the same logic to *just* today's data. In fact, I have done this on quite a few occasions.

However, the longer you keep at this, the more often you will see the same products listed, and the more information you can aggregate to estimate your equilibrium prices more accurately. You will end up constructing a graph more like the previous ones, showing multiple data points over time, and allowing for a more confident estimation of the average asking price and resulting equilibrium point.

Optimizing Data Analysis on Craigslist

Now that you have the basics of price analysis down, I will tell you about a very powerful way to put your research on autopilot via automatic alerts.

What I'm about to tell you is one of my best-kept secrets. It's a great way to keep an eye out for deals without actively researching items. Moreover, it's based on the exact keywords you specify, so you can make it as narrow or broad as you wish.

The way it works is to automatically notify you anytime an item with certain keywords is posted to Craigslist. Wouldn't it be nice to have a simple alert pop up on your phone anytime such an item is listed, showing the post title and price? It certainly makes information gathering much easier. Best of all, you can set these alerts up to arrive via email, text message, android/iPhone alerts, and more. It's all up to you.

To get started, go to www.ifttt.com and setup an account. IFTTT stands for "If this, then that" in case you were wondering.

Once you create your account and login, the interface is fairly self-explanatory. Your goal is to create a "recipe" that programs some aspect of your life, in this case the process of knowing when a particular Craigslist posting is made. To give you a sneak peak of what your recipe will look like when it's finished, here's a screenshot of my home screen:

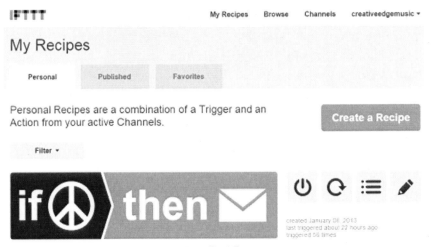

E-mails me anytime someone puts a Mesa Dual Rec up for sale on Craigslist.

Quick reminder: When you turn a Recipe off then back on, it resets as if you had just created it.

Here you can see I've been using a recipe that emails me anytime a Mesa Dual Rec (a type of guitar amplifier) is posted on Craigslist. This is what the notification emails look like in my gmail inbox:

Inbox Mesa dual rec tremoverb (Round rock) $850 - email.ifttt.com/wf/click?upn=jGHDfwvrKDxaof	Sep 15
Inbox 1988 Washburn J6 Hollowbody Jazz Electric (NE Austin) $800 - email.ifttt.com/wf/click?upn=	Sep 9
Inbox Mesa Boogie Dual Rectifier Head (Austin) $1000 - email.ifttt.com/wf/click?upn=jGHDfwvrKD:	Sep 1
Inbox Epiphone SG w/ EMG 81/85 (La Mesa) $275 - email.ifttt.com/wf/click?upn=jGHDfwvrKDxao	Aug 9
Inbox Mesa Boogie Stiletto Deuce Amp Head (Ramona) $950 - email.ifttt.com/wf/click?upn=jGHDf	Jul 30
Inbox Mesa Boogie Dual Rectifier (3 Channel) $1100 - email.ifttt.com/wf/click?upn=jGHDfwvrKDxa	May 7
Inbox Mesa Boogie dual rec tremoverb head $100 - email.ifttt.com/wf/click?upn=jGHDfwvrKDxaofc	Apr 27
Inbox Price lowered : Mesa Boogie multi-watts Dual rec half stack (South San Diego) $1499 - ema	Mar 12
Inbox Mesa Boogie Express 5:25 plus 12"Mint FS Ft (Downtown) $800 - email.ifttt.com/wf/click?up	Mar 11

While IFTTT allows for a multitude of notification methods, the reason I prefer email is because I can accumulate multiple data points over time and review them all together like in the above screenshot. Plus, I get pinged on my phone anytime a new email comes in, so it doubles as a real-time alert.

Creating a recipe to notify you of a Craigslist posting couldn't be easier. Once you login, you'll arrive at the "Create a Recipe" page.

Start by clicking the "this" hyperlink, which automatically takes you to a screen where you get to define "this." In our case, we will be selecting the Craigslist Trigger Channel.

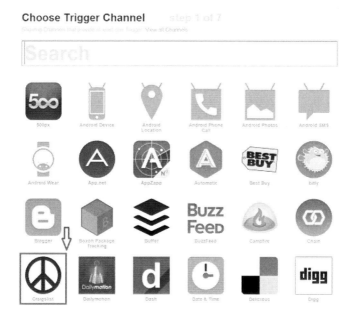

Once Craigslist is selected, you will be prompted to choose a specific Trigger.

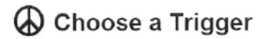

☮ Choose a Trigger

New post from search
Copy and paste the URL from the
results page of any search on
Craigslist and this Trigger fires every
time someone adds a new post that
meets the search criteria.

You will then need to post the URL from a specific Craigslist search into the "Search results URL" box. Simply go to Craigslist, perform a search for a given item, and then copy and paste the URL from your address bar into this box. In this case, you can see I've conducted a search for the keyword "tube amplifier."

ebay **Complete Trigger Fields**   step 3 of 7

New item from search

ebay **Search terms**

Sound Diffuser

What are you searching for on eBay?

ebay **Max price**

Optional

Create Trigger

Now it's time to define "that."

New post from search Search
URL

This brings us to our set of choices for our Action Channel:

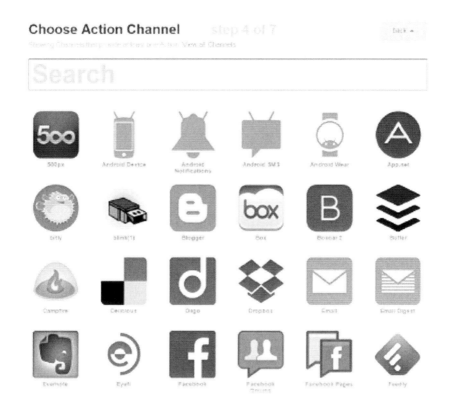

At this point, choose the notification method you'd like to use and finish creating your recipe. From here forward, unless you pause your recipe from within your account, IFTTT will execute it periodically (I believe the interval is set to every 15 minutes) and notify you via your Action Channel when your specified criterion is met.

Congratulations – you have created an automated "drip campaign" that feeds you real-time market information! In addition to the benefit of getting familiar with product pricing, this will also allow you to capitalize on deals faster. Since you will be notified very soon after a new posting is made, you will have the unique opportunity to be first in line to respond to the seller.

In my experience, sellers tend to get excited when people respond to their listings right away. Doing so might increase your opportunity of getting the seller to agree to a lower offer, too, since at that point in time they may be uncertain about future prospects. Do they risk losing the bird in hand for a better offer in the bush?

Not to mention, being prompt puts you in a great position to capitalize on rare deals where sellers list their items way under market value. Since those deals are bound to get snatched up right away, it's all but required that you be the first person to respond to the listing and set an appointment.

My recommendation is to make several recipes spanning all of your niche's keywords. Armed with this new tool, you will always be first in line; it will be everyone else who shows up to the party just a bit too late.

How Item Condition Factors In

Now that I have thoroughly exhausted your brain, let's look at another factor that comes into play frequently enough to deserve a discussion: the condition of an item. We would hope that all used products would be "as good as new," but of course, this is not always the case, and especially not on Craigslist.

Namely, you may need to adjust your target sales price down for a particular item if it is flawed. Maybe it was repaired at some point, has a cosmetic issue, or a serious functional problem. Think about whether or not these flaws are trivial, and whether they are things the average person would require a repair on either before or after purchasing from you, and how that would affect your bottom line. The actual amount of the resulting price adjustment you might make is a matter of individual judgment.

Adjusting your target sales price down for a given item also means you will be offering less when purchasing it. This is a perfectly reasonable expectation. You cannot sell an item with flaws or cosmetic issues for as much as an item without those issues. Therefore, you should get a price break when purchasing a flawed item. More than once, I have gone as far as obtaining a repair quote to more accurately identify the necessary price adjustment and passing the quote onto the seller when making my offer.

One time, I even took a seller and his product to a local guitar store to speak with my usual guitar tech, so he could provide an impartial, third-party opinion regarding the condition and playability of an acoustic guitar that had a warped neck.

For the record, I do not recommend investing this type of time on all of your deals, but occasionally extreme measures like this are okay! Just make sure there will be enough profit in the deal to cover your time. Here is the story:

The product was a Taylor 110 acoustic guitar, and it was a truly beautiful guitar, but the seller who owned it probably had the wrong gauge strings on there for way too long, and they pulled the neck out of shape. It was either that or the truss rod inside the guitar was not set at the right tension. Regardless, the neck was not straight. In layman's terms, there was a flaw.

The seller argued that the neck was fine and that I had nothing to worry about. But, having played guitars for fifteen years and being very sensitive to microscopic issues with playability, I picked up on it right away and there was nothing he could have said to convince me otherwise.

I told him it was not the guitar for me, and that unfortunately I would not be able to pay the price we had agreed to previously. After all, I had agreed to buy a guitar that was in good operating condition at the negotiated price, and now I had discovered that it was not in good operating condition.

The seller asked if there was anything we could work out, and that is when I suggested we go to the guitar store. I called the shop to see if my usual tech was there, and fortunately he was, so I spoke to him about it over the phone. He said he was available at the moment if we wanted to bring the guitar down for him to evaluate. Hence, I made the following suggestion to the seller of the guitar.

The basic deal was that if my tech could fix it quickly and easily at no cost, then I would honor my original price. Otherwise, if there was a repair involved, then the repair would come straight off the top of the price.

After my tech looked at the guitar, he said it needed a $50 repair plus new strings. The new strings and restringing would be another $25 or so. I agreed to suck up the cost of the new strings myself if the seller took the $50off of his asking price. He took the deal and I picked the guitar up the following week after the repair was completed. All in all, I was into the purchase for $315.

I ended up selling that guitar for $425, which was exactly $110 higher than what I paid including the repair and strings. Ironically, the model number of the guitar was 110. It was meant to be! It felt good to improve a used instrument and put it back into the market in better condition than when I received it, too.

Generally speaking, do not shy away from flawed items. Buying damaged or entirely broken products can actually be really profitable. You will typically buy them at a huge discount, repair them for a very small sum of money, and then capture larger profits than normal in your resale.

The best example of this stems from a resale one of my friends organized. He purchased a broken PA system for $350 with the thought of fixing it up and reselling it. In the end, it only cost him $50 to repair the horn that was broken on one of the speakers, and he went on to quickly resell the PA system for $900. In a matter of just two weeks, he turned a $500 profit by handling a simple repair mess that the previous owner was too impatient to deal with. This is a real case of one man's trash becoming another man's treasure!

You can easily form relationships with local repairmen and contractors who can take the things you purchase and fix them up. The resulting value added may often be more than what you had to pay for the fix. This is yet another opportunity for profit beyond the usual hustle, and it might even make you feel good to know that you are up-cycling used goods and putting them back to work in society.

What Does it Cost New?

One final factor to consider when evaluating a product's potential Equilibrium Price is the price it sells for *new*. For discontinued items, this can be harder to determine, but Google makes it simple enough to locate historical price information.

Epiphone Les Paul Standards go for about $500 new

The new price of an item gives you an idea of what the manufacturer and distributors think the product is worth and may help guide your intuition a bit. If you see an item selling for way lower than its new price, it could be an indication of a deal. Conversely, items selling fairly close to their new prices tend not to be such good deals; the argument "it's only a little more to buy one new" tends to come into play, and makes it harder to complete a sale.

Here is another feature of knowing the new, retail price of your items: depending on the niche you are in, you may eventually notice a pattern by which used items sell at a predictable percentage of their new price. If so, this pattern or percentage can be used to help you more quickly evaluate future deals. This can be especially helpful when there are few data points available for analysis, as we discussed previously.

In the musical equipment niche, I've found that most used items sell in the range of 40-80% of their new price, depending on the item. For instance, Epiphone Les Paul Standards go for $500 brand new. As you know, I have sold three of them at $350+ with hard cases. Without the hard cases, they might have sold for $300 each, and $300 / $500 = 60%. This 60% is right in the middle of that 40-80% range I have identified, and helps solidify my belief that this range is accurate. Even with the hard cases (which cost about $80 new), $350 / $580 = 60%, also at the same mark.

As you accumulate your own sales data, you will eventually get a feel for the *percentages* at which most of your items sell. This will in turn strengthen your ability to identify potentially undervalued items in the future. In my case, whenever I see musical equipment selling for less than about half of its new price, I know there is a good chance I can turn it into a profitable deal. At least it's one more "positive indicator."

But even without any experience selling a particular item, we have already seen how knowing the new price can still provide very useful information. In my experience, *the lower an item sells for on the used market compared to its new price, the more potential it has for profitable resale.* This is because there is a degree of subjectivity when pricing used items, and that subjectivity tends to vary more where there is higher depreciation. Ultimately, this allows for greater price fluctuations to exist, which can be leveraged as both a buyer and a seller.

For example, I have seen plenty of products that sell for around $600 new but go for around $300 on the used market. Because of the large depreciation factor (50%), there tends to be a fairly wide array of resulting sales prices. Folks trying to move the product quickly may list as low as $200, while others might hold out for the buyer willing to pay up to $400 for that same item in good condition. Being on the right end of those deals is key to capturing profits.

On the other hand, some items may depreciate less (usually high-value items) and those items will tend to sell closer to their original retail prices. One stereo compressor I purchased a while back retails for $1,800 new, but tends to sell around $1,300 used – only a 27% depreciation factor (as compared to the 50% described above). I bought mine for $1,130 and resold it for $1,320 – a $190 gain, but just a 14.39% profit margin due to the narrower degree of price fluctuations. It would have been difficult for me to find one any cheaper than I did (they retain their value well), and similarly tough to sell any higher (any higher and someone might opt for a new one with a warranty, for instance).

Working the Functional Price Range

The last few paragraphs introduce us to the concept of the **functional price range** (FPR), which is the spectrum of prices from low to high that we can actually expect to see sales occur at in the used market. This is useful to know, since it gives us an idea of just how low we can expect to buy, and how high we might pull off a sale.

Once you have identified an estimate for your equilibrium price, it is possible to incorporate information such as the item's new price and your profit threshold to mathematically estimate your FPR – I lay out a detailed method for this in Appendix D.

However, the "regular" way of determining your FPR is by simply observing the difference between the highest and lowest asking prices observed, then knocking those boundaries down a bit to account for negotiation, like we normally do when adjusting average asking prices down to estimate Equilibrium. You can apply a little intuition, as well, but generally speaking, hard data will be most reliable. Here's what this might look like:

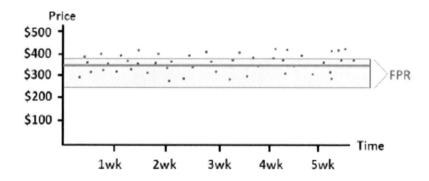

Having already accounted for your equilibrium price, you come up with the FPR (the grey box) by moving it down a bit from where it would normally entrap most or all data points. Normally, your equilibrium price will be towards the higher end of your FPR, a bit below the upper boundary.

This reflects the fact that you do intend to "play the price range" to your advantage, but without pushing your luck too much. Of course, when it actually comes time to create a sales listing and choose an asking price, you should place your asking price a little above equilibrium and potentially even above the upper boundary of your FPR – you never know what might happen (quite honestly, I do tend to post many of my listings a good bit above what I plan to actually sell at). However, if you do this, expect to negotiate with buyers more, and realize that some buyers may not contact you at all if they think your price is simply beyond their means.

Now you might question me, "Steve, wasn't I supposed to Sell *Low*? If I'm selling at the higher end of the FPR, how is that low?"

Well, it *is* low. Low in the sense that your actual, target sales price is *competitive* within the market. Plus, you are still likely undercutting others who are posting even higher than you.

The questioning might continue, "But there are still data points lower than mine – asking prices that are less. How will I be able to sell?"

Here I will remind you to step back and look at the big picture. In order to be profitable, you *do* need to buy at prices that are lower than you sell. Hence, there will necessarily be a gap between the lowest observed prices and the prices you need to sell at. This does mean you will *not* be the lowest price the Craigslist world has ever seen. You might be on any given day, but you might not, and that's okay.

Think about it: if you were to sell at the absolute lowest end of the FPR, your profit threshold would dictate that you need to buy at a price so silly that it's unlikely to ever happen (okay, well it might happen on occasion – but such windfalls should not be relied on). In layman's terms, if you aim *too* low on the sales side, it will be difficult or impossible to find purchasing opportunities that allow for any profit to be made.

The game, then, is learning to play the FPR just right. Ideally, you will be the buyer at those lowest of prices, and be the seller at the highest of them. More likely, you will fall somewhere in between on both, but by keeping towards the edges of the FPR boundaries, you can still set yourself up for a good profit.

Interpretation

Despite all the math and academic concepts we have covered in this chapter so far, you should know that estimating an equilibrium price is just as much an art as it is a science. To be even more straightforward, it is a hustle. It means doing some reasonable data analysis to shield against needless loss, then rolling the dice and keeping your fingers crossed that you come out ahead.

This is similar, albeit on a smaller scale, to how Wall Street guys and gals gamble on market movements. They use incredibly complex mathematics to figure out what might happen next and minimize risk. Most of them are very smart people, too. But they can't predict the future, and sometimes (perhaps even frequently), they are wrong.

Every now and then, some hotshot thinks they have finally come up with a bulletproof algorithm to "crack the code," but all such algorithms eventually fail to some degree, and some are rendered obsolete altogether. For a good read on the subject, pick up a copy of *The Intelligent Investor* by Benjamin Graham, who was Warren Buffet's mentor.

The math and algorithms do still help, though, which is why stock traders will use a system complete with its imperfections – even if it fails them sometimes, it may be their best shot at victory.

My system is not completely bulletproof, either, but one big advantage to transacting business on Craigslist (as opposed to Wall Street) is that the market is much, much smaller. You see, stocks on Wall Street are pushed by voluminous market forces to a single price at any point in time – which is clearly advertised, and at which no buyer would pay a penny more and no seller would accept a penny less.

On Craigslist, though, there are few enough buyers and sellers in the market at any given time that we can more easily find **arbitrage opportunities**. Arbitrage is defined as the "simultaneous" buying and selling of securities, inventory, or other assets in order to gain a profit resulting from differences in price related to market inefficiencies.

In fact, this is the entire premise of earning a profit on Craigslist – we are leveraging the fact that the market *is* relatively inefficient, with varying prices for identical items and a resulting price range that can be "played" at both ends. These inefficiencies help us minimize risk, too, and at least with my system, I have encountered very little loss as a result.

Purchasing at the Right Time

While much of purchasing falls into line on its own once you determine an equilibrium price and analyze your FPR (read: wait to buy until you can pick up the item in question at the price you have determined is beneficial), it is still helpful to keep the following information in mind to maximize your success.

Create "Good Timing" with Volume

It is often said that we pick up great deals when we happen to be "in the right place at the right time." How can we make sure we are in the right place at the right time, then, when that seller who is comfortable selling at the low end of the FPR shows up with his or her listing?

Setting up automated notifications via IFTTT is your best shot, but even if you are using this service to notify you of new listings in real time, you should still be checking the listings the "old fashioned way" on a regular basis (i.e., log on to the Craigslist home page and conduct a search). Otherwise, you might be missing out on key deals that aren't part of your automated drip campaign.

Then, when browsing the listings and identifying items you'd like to buy, you must *mass email* sellers with offers that allow you to meet your profit threshold.

The easiest way to do this is to simply search for a specific product, and then quickly email your offer to all sellers with current listings. Here is an example of the language I might use:

> *"Hi, I'm interested in your (ITEM). I could offer you $X if you can drop it off in (MY AREA). Please let me know, thanks!*
>
> *-Steve*
> *(555) 555-5555"*

Alternatively, if you really feel like you're low-balling the person:

"Hey there, I'm interested in your (ITEM). I could offer you $X if you can drop it off in (MY AREA). I know this is a bit lower than what you are asking, but please keep me in mind if you don't get any better offers. Thx!

-Steve
(555) 555-5555"

In both cases, you can add your phone number to show the other person you're a serious buyer. This might sound silly, but it really does lead to more responses.

Finally, my personal favorite:

"Hey, I have $X cash in hand right now if you can drop off (ITEM) in (MY AREA) in the near future. Let me know, thx!"

-Steve
(555) 555-5555"

The subtle difference here is the use of the word "cash." The fact that you have "cash in hand" might seem like a silly distinction to make, when all of us should expect most transactions on Craigslist to be cash deals. However, the reference to cold, hard money can be a powerful motivator – especially when someone needs liquid currency fast – and rules out the possibility that you might offer something for trade, which is a surprisingly frequent occurrence.

Another difference with this particular wording is that we are also moving the price closer up to the beginning of the email, making it seem more important.

Note that for any given item up for sale, there may only be a few people selling one at any point in time. Since you may need to send out 8-12 emails to get a solid response or two, you'll need to make offers on quite a few different items at a time to reach a critical mass and find sellers who are agreeable to your offers, or willing to negotiate at the very least.

Times of Day, Month, and Year

In this section, I'd like to share with you some insights that have helped me identify sellers who are more likely to negotiate their prices down – and are thus better targets when I'm the buyer. There are some complimentary insights on the sales side here, too.

The first point is to take note of the *time of day* a listing is posted. For a long time, I never paid attention to this, but one day I discovered why I should tune into it.

Postings made during normal business hours and the early evening are the "norm" and do not necessarily reflect anything special. Someone is listing their item for sale – great.

What might a late night posting—between 11:00 pm and 3:00 am — mean, though? Well, it could just mean that the person is a night owl or, if it's during the summer, perhaps it's a teenager who is on break from school and in the habit of staying up all night. On the other hand, it might mean that the seller is in a hurry to sell because they need cash for something important. After all, if this is a time when someone would normally be asleep, why would they be up late posting things for sale on Craigslist unless they have a specific financial goal in mind?

Perhaps they owe someone money, are trying to round up a few bucks before a soon-approaching vacation, or are hoping to get some cash to purchase an item from someone else on Craigslist. It stands to reason that, under such circumstances, many people will be more willing to negotiate on price, since their financial goal is focused on something other than the item they are selling.

The next point to take note of is *time of the month*. People pay their bills at different times, but it seems to me that many folks have rent or mortgage payments due at or near the start of the month. When items go up for sale within the last few days of the month, it may be a sign that someone is trying to get that last bit of cash they need to cover their bill. Listings made on the 1st, 2nd, or 3rd of the month that are OBO (or best offer) listings and are already priced competitively definitely grab my attention – and all the more when the seller indicates a need or desire to sell quickly in his/her listing.

Last but not least, there are *time of year* considerations. In chronological order, I find good deals posted in March by people who are spring cleaning; in May/June by people looking to raise money for summer vacations; and in late November/early December by people trying to raise some cash before the holidays – perhaps to purchase gifts for others, or make travel arrangements.

Speaking of time of year considerations, there are a few on the sales side, too. Ask yourself, when are buyers in your market more likely to have extra cash to purchase things they *want*?

The last week of December is a toss-up with so many people out of town, but with many people receiving bonuses and financial gifts from work, family, and friends before and during the holidays, they may be "on the hunt" to buy that shiny new item you have for sale. Similarly, starting in late March/early April and running through May, many Americans will get their tax refunds from the federal government – and many will spend that money on personal satisfaction/enjoyment, not limited to but potentially including your inventory. Finally, the summer months can occasionally be lucrative, with college kids out of school and looking for hobbies to spend their time and money on.

It makes sense, then, to be "stocked up" with good inventory for these times of year, if at all possible.

The tips in this section fall into the category of "advanced prospecting," in the sense that we are incorporating a more sophisticated level of detail into our purchasing (and sales) efforts. They are not fool-proof by any means, and will not always be a trustworthy guide, but still may serve as indicators that will help you in your quest to be profitable.

Exploring alternative markets where the time is always right

As a final point on buying at the right time, you might wish to consider some alternative, non-Craigslist markets for acquiring new inventory from time to time – markets where it's *always* a good time to buy, since the nature of the market is one of steep discounts.

Events such as estate sales, garage and yard sales, and builder's model home liquidations fall into this category and can be a gold mine.

Along the same lines, you can go directly to a liquidator to look for deals – these are people who themselves are in the business of "flipping" for a profit, purchasing goods from manufacturers or distributors for pennies, then selling them to you and me for more. But don't let this discourage you, as there can still be significant room for profit on the back end for you.

Liquidators can be found anywhere and everywhere, and often the local guy is best. There are plenty of liquidators to be found online, as well. Take Walmart's liquidation auction site, for example: https://liquidations.walmart.com/

Walmart.com
Mixed Lots

Walmart.com
Furniture

Outdoor Living, Home Decor and more, 12 Double Pallets. Over 26K Retail, Johnstown, NY (9196)

Current Bid: **$1,254**

Bids: 6

Closes in 17h 25m

Furniture and more, 12 Double Pallets. Over 22K Retail, Johnstown, NY (9196)

Current Bid: **$2,650**

Bids: 12

Closes in 17h 30m

Some listings, such as the ones shown here, might only make sense for someone with ample storage space, but if you do have the space, it can pay off in the long run. Moreover, there are plenty of opportunities that are not in such bulk, and can be more easily managed by an individual operating on a casual basis.

In general, exploiting alternative markets like these may bring you "out of your niche" here and there, but can be a profitable pursuit worthy of making the exception from time to time. One of my friends makes his living by acquiring inventory in such markets and reselling it on eBay, and there are plenty more folks just like him taking advantage of these acquisition opportunities every day.

Therefore, despite the main focus in this chapter on Craigslist, it is worth dropping by the occasional garage sale or estate sale to explore the available loot – you never know what you might find.

Chapter 6 Recap

- Sell Low and Buy *Lower*.
- Understand the basics of supply and demand.
- Look for patterns in product asking prices to spot more deals.
- Estimate your *equilibrium price* and *functional price range* from current and historical market data.
- Embrace items in need of repair, rather than running from them.
- Purchase when the time is right, taking note of the potential meanings of listings made at certain times of the day, month, and year.

If, for any reason, the graphs, terms, or explanations in this chapter seemed a little complicated, that is perfectly okay. You absolutely do not need to draw graphs, invest crazy amounts of time doing price research, or perform math equations to be successful. Most of the in-depth explanation set forth in this chapter was done simply to thoroughly explain the underlying thought processes and principles behind this part of my system. In practice, all this fancy stuff boils down to a very simple process that happens as you analyze the market.

At any given time, one Craigslist search and one eBay search is all I do when getting price comps, and it takes me a whopping two to three minutes, at the most, to do this. In addition, I spend five minutes scanning the listings every day or two, which gives my brain the chance to record and analyze a large amount of data on an ongoing basis. I tell you this to put it all in perspective, because this chapter might give the impression that hours of research will be necessary to succeed. This could not be further from the truth. Most of my deals result from an incredibly small time investment of five minutes or less.

Assignments

1. Re-read this chapter at least once to solidify the ideas set forth within. This is one of the most important functional chapters of the book, as it covers the purchasing and resale process in detail, along with the logic behind it. It is crucial that you clearly understand how this works in order to succeed.

2. Pick three products in your niche and do a little research on pricing. Look at Craigslist and eBay to see where other sellers are pricing these products, making note of these numbers. Find out the price these items sell for new, too. This process should not take more than 5-10 minutes for all three products chosen. Continue checking up on these products every few days for the next several weeks. Identify your equilibrium price for these products, and in doing so, determine the price you would be comfortable buying these products at in order to obtain a profit in resale.

On Deck

In the next chapter, we will break free of the "technical" and get back to the "creative" by exploring calculated risk taking, which ultimately boils down to having the *cajones* to strike when the iron is hot. As powerful as it is to perform quantitative analysis, so too is it vital to confidently take action when the time is right.

7

ROLL THE DICE

HOW I EARNED $935 IN JUST TWO DEALS

In order to make great deals, you have to be motivated to take calculated risks. While the last chapter focused on price analytics, this chapter is all about execution.

Preparation
Planning & Measuring
Deal Analysis
Purchasing
Sales

You can be brilliant with price analysis but still fail if you do not embrace the inherent risk-taking that comes with entrepreneurship. You must confidently take action on both purchases and sales when the time is right and follow through with your underlying plans until they are complete.

Taking action in a swift manner does not come naturally to everyone, at least not in business. With so many variables to consider, along with the underlying risk involved in business deals, it is easy for us to shy away from decisively moving forward with a deal. What if I lose money? What if this deal is not the right move for me? What if I have miscalculated?

These types of questions reflect a certain amount of justifiable caution. However, they must be momentary, objective questions that you quickly and quietly answer to yourself before moving forward with prompt action. If you are dwelling on these types of questions often, it reflects a hindering level of self-doubt that must be addressed. If this is you, revisit Chapter 2, where we discussed overcoming fear of failure and introduced the concept of embracing risks.

Please know I am very much in favor of being cautious, doing the math, and making intelligent business decisions. This is absolutely necessary and vital to long-term success, and is precisely what the last chapter covered in detail. But at the same time, you must marry "number crunching" with "action taking" to get anywhere with all that analysis. Otherwise, you can spend significant time analyzing deals without ever realizing the benefit of your analysis.

I always aim to work efficiently, operate with a high level of self-confidence, and trust my intuition when evaluating deals. Note, this includes shutting deals down right away when my intuition gives me a clear signal that the deal is no good. However, when I sense my "Intelligent Decision-Making" side trying to shut down a potentially profitable deal simply because of a little uncertainty or doubt, I let my "Risk-Taking Mentality" dominate for the sake of keeping both cash and inventory moving. The following graph illustrates how this works in practice:

This illustration reflects the fact that both extremes are fundamental to the process, but that your Risk-Taking Mentality should win when you are torn between the two. For example, perhaps your Risk-Taking Mentality is excited about a deal and feels it will be a great opportunity, but your Intelligent Decision-Making side is not sure enough information is available to confirm future profitability. Rather than walking away from the deal in this situation, I would recommend going out on a limb and seeing what happens.

I know this sounds a bit arbitrary and risky, but frankly, if you always err on the side of caution, you will slow your momentum and walk away from too many great opportunities.

Intelligent Decision-Making is surely important, but you can reach a stalemate, wherein you take *no* action, if you allow yourself to run in endless circles considering all the possibilities, doubting every deal for some small reason or another. Remember, there are tools in Chapter 2 that can be used to address this type of hang-up.

My system simply does not work unless you are actually *using* the system, and you must get comfortable with the idea of making decisions with less-than-perfect information in order to reap its benefits.

Let me give you a case in point to show how putting myself on the line in a particular situation turned into one of my best deals ever.

The Universal Accordion Story

Until recently, I did not know very much about accordions. Why, then, was I compelled one night to hop in my car and race more than twenty miles down the freeway (breaking one of my own rules!) to pick one up from someone on Craigslist? Well, I did it because there was an opportunity like no other, or so it seemed. Here is how it all happened.

One night, I flipped up the screen on my laptop to check out the new listings on Craigslist. As I scrolled through the listings, I noticed one for a "Universal Accordion." At first, I was not sure if the word "Universal" was a brand name or simply a representation that this accordion functioned according to some universal standard. I have since learned that Universal *is* in fact a brand name.

Anyway, this particular Universal Accordion was listed for a mere $100, so I thought, "What the heck, let's see what this thing looks like."

To my surprise, the picture in the ad showed a beautiful, brilliant accordion. I was not really qualified to know what "beautiful" looked like for an accordion, but something told me that this thing was in really good shape, and probably worth a *lot* more than $100.

But I reminded myself that I did not know jack squat about accordions, and that I might be wasting my time on something completely useless. Maybe it was worth nothing and I was just caught up in a silly dream. Thus, instead of picking up the phone and calling the seller, I just sent a short email, asking if they would be able to drop it off at my house the next day.

I went back to watching television for a short while, but that darn accordion kept popping back into my head. I said to myself, "That accordion really did look super nice. Heck, for just $100, it might really be worth checking out. If nothing else, it might be a fun thing to keep!"

The next thing I did really freaked me out. I went on eBay to see if anyone else was selling Universal Accordions to get a better idea of what this one might *really* be worth. Once I hit the search button, I was blown away to see one listed for $1,479. Here is a screenshot of the exact item I saw.

Universal (Guerrini) Accordion/Accordian, Dry Tuning, Excellent Condition

Top Rated Plus

$1,479.00
Buy It Now

What I realized was this Universal Accordion on eBay looked *exactly* like the one I had seen listed on Craigslist. Oh my god.

Now, before I go any further, let me put this in perspective for you. This listing is still up on eBay almost a year later, so clearly nobody has purchased this accordion for $1,479. Plus, when I originally saw this, something told me this eBay listing had probably been up for a while already by the time I viewed it.

But still, if *someone* valued this same exact instrument at over a thousand dollars, I knew the one for sale in San Diego that night must be worth more than $100.

I picked up the phone immediately.

It was getting late, and the lady who owned the accordion was getting ready for bed in an hour. I asked if there was any way I could pay her an extra $25 on top of her asking price to come pick it up within the hour. She agreed and gave me her address.

When I arrived, she showed me the accordion and told me its entire history. She had been the original owner since 1964 and had taken impressive care of her instrument. The accordion had been used in local parades, certain recordings, and more. She informed me that it was made in Italy and was a highly sought-after model.

The accordion came with a hard case, too. She even went so far as to tell me that it had recently been appraised for more than $500, but she did not want to deal with consigning it or waiting too long for the right buyer, which was why she had listed it for $100. She was in the process of moving and was simply looking to move it onto a new home and clear some space in her garage.

After bringing it home, I waited a week or two to list it for sale. I wanted to give myself some time to play with it and let some of my friends and band mates fool around with it, too. We had some really fun times simply attempting to get the straps on, hold the thing upright, and construct a few basic melodies. The thought of keeping it bounced around a few times, but in the end, my friends reached the same conclusion that I did: none of us really knew how to play it, nor were we going to use it for any particular purpose, such as recording, anytime soon.

Therefore, I took some really good shots of the accordion with my camera phone and listed it for $650, a price that I thought was a little on the low end, given the condition, but still representative of a healthy profit.

The finish on the Universal Accordion was impeccable

The very next morning I got an email from a gentleman located in Tijuana, Mexico who was extremely interested. He offered me $600 and said he wanted to take a look at it and play it before buying. I agreed to meet him the same day so he could check it out.

Within minutes of the gentleman's arrival, I could tell he liked the accordion very much. He spoke little English, so we conversed mostly in Spanish (I can get through basic conversations in Spanish alright), but even then, the conversation was minimal. He pretty much just put the accordion on, started playing some tunes (quite well, I might add!), and decided very quickly that this would be the one for him.

The sale closed at $600 as agreed, and in less than a week I had made $455. Note, the $455 is calculated from deducting the purchase price of $125*and* $20 in gas/mileage to pick up this accordion. It was a huge profit, and while I was really sad to see such a great instrument go, I was happy that I was generating some serious cash. Now I could do more to build out our recording studio and potentially buy up some more inventory to keep the upward spiral going.

The really crazy thing is how quickly I found the *next* accordion, also in great shape and being sold for an incredibly cheap price.

The Crucianelli Accordion Story

Right after selling the Universal accordion, I had the keen idea to find another accordion just like it and duplicate the process. My thought was that if I could do it once, I could do it again, and I was absolutely right.

Within a couple of weeks, I found a beautiful, red Crucianelli accordion on Craigslist that was in really great shape.

The listing price was right around $150, so I offered $120 to the seller and he accepted it right away. Before agreeing to meet up, though, I made sure to ask the standard questions about its history, his reasons for selling it, and the current condition, including any flaws or damage. Apparently, the gentleman had acquired this accordion several years back after a family member passed away and was tired of it taking up space.

He stated he knew it was likely worth quite a bit more than he was asking, but that he was not so concerned with the financial component of the sale. He mentioned that I was the first person to make an offer on the accordion, despite his listing being up for more than a week, and he wanted to move it along as soon as possible. There was no price negotiation, simply a hurried request by the seller to meet up and complete the transaction.

The fact that he was in such a hurry raised a small red flag at first, and I considered that there might be something wrong with the accordion that I would not be able to identify due to my lack of experience in that area. However, my gut told me to go with it and at least meet up with him to check it out. After all, he had already offered to drive out to my place as soon as we were off the phone. I told him that I would certainly be willing to look at it and pay the $120 if everything seemed in good order.

Less than half an hour later, the gentleman pulled up on my street and I met him at the curb. He opened his trunk, opened the case to the accordion, and took the accordion out to show me what it looked like. It truly was very beautiful and I could tell it had been maintained well throughout the years, despite a thin layer of dust that had collected from sitting idle in his garage for so long.

I tested out a few notes to make sure everything sounded alright, had a short conversation with the seller about my recording studio, and eventually purchased the accordion for $120. Then I got my sales listing up just a few days later at $650.

The difference between this accordion and the last one was the amount of time it took to find a buyer. I had a few offers come in for $250, $350, and even as much as $450 that I turned down almost immediately. After seeing the Universal accordion sell for $600, I was holding out for something higher. The person who offered $450 did get my gears turning, though, and I wrote back to say that, if I did not get a better offer in the near future, I might be willing to accept it.

Fortunately, just a week or two later, I received an email from a college student who seemed very interested. Price was not discussed, but he was eager to arrange a meeting to try it out and potentially buy it. In my experience, when someone does not try to negotiate price up front and goes out of their way to drive out for a meeting, they are expecting to pay full price or close to it.

It turned out that this particular young man was trying to find an accordion for his father, so his father came to the meeting, too. The father was originally from Japan and did not speak English, which was why his son needed to broker the deal. I could tell he really liked the accordion and wanted to buy it, but I did not understand exactly what the son and father were discussing in their native language. It seemed like there was a bit of hesitation, or perhaps a discussion taking place regarding the price.

Eventually the son asked if I would be willing to negotiate on price, and I indicated that I would be happy to take off $50 and accept a total of $600. Another short foreign language discussion took place, and then the kid told me they had only brought $500 with them to the meeting.

I held firm on my price of $600 and communicated that it was the absolute best I could do. I explained where the nearest banks and ATMs were for most of the major branches (this is good to know, by the way, in case it ever comes up during a meeting), and told them I would be happy to wait another half-hour for them to return with the full payment. However, I pointed out that I legitimately had plans after that and would not be able to meet with them until a later time if we could not wrap this up soon.

They hemmed and hawed for a minute or two, but when I started turning the lights off and closing up shop, they finally arrived at the decision that they would run to the bank and get the extra $100. They left for the bank and indicated they would be back in no more than half an hour.

Twenty-five minutes later, I received a call from the kid stating that they were still at the bank and unsure about the purchase. They had not withdrawn the money yet and were starting to think about pulling out of the deal.

I calmly explained that I would be more than okay with it if they walked away, but that I did need to get going so I was not late to my next appointment. If they were not back in the next five minutes, I would be leaving and might end up selling the accordion to someone else if I received a full price offer in the near future.

This was a bit of a bluff, but I felt it best here to use the common tactic of *setting a false time constraint* to motivate them to action. Whether it's a coupon that's about to expire, a sale scheduled to end on a certain day, or another type of "last chance" offer, these can be very effective, since they artificially stimulate a sense of impending loss – and as we discussed in Chapter 2, loss aversion is a powerful thing.

After fifteen seconds of silence on the other end, the kid finally confirmed they were withdrawing the money and should be back in the next five minutes. Sure enough, they showed up five minutes later and paid the agreed price of $600. They thanked me for waiting and seemed very happy with the acquisition, offering to send me a picture of the accordion once it reached its new home.

This deal netted a total profit of $480, even better than the Universal accordion. Between the two deals, I generated $935 in total profit. There was some risk in purchasing these accordions, and even some risk during the sales process with the Crucianelli, since the father and son almost walked away from the deal. However, the risk was necessary to reap the reward.

Lessons Learned

Calculated risks can and do pay off. They will not *always* pay off by any means. But they do go well from time to time, and if you take enough risks, you are bound to enjoy the success that comes with the habit.

Of course, I must encourage you to also be calculating, analytical, and smart about your risks and gambles. Research must still be done to get an idea of what something is worth before you purchase it.

However, there is a point where the calculations end and your gut instinct must take over. If you get too caught up in "What if I can't sell it," "What if it takes a long time to sell," "I don't know how I feel about putting money into this," or "I don't have enough information to know this is a guaranteed thing," it will prevent you from moving out of your comfort zone and rolling the dice once in a while.

I believe the greatest successes in life come when we put ourselves outside of our comfort zones. Once you start putting yourself outside your comfort zone on a regular basis, you will soon discover very precisely where the optimal blend of "Intelligent Decision-Making" and "Risk-Taking Mentality" lies. You will calibrate yourself to know the exact moment when enough is enough on the cerebral side and exactly when to move into taking action.

Make the commitment to put yourself outside of your comfort zone and take a little risk. Beyond getting more involved with your deals on Craigslist, you can practice this in other ways. Take up a new fitness routine, flirt with an attractive member of the opposite sex (if you are single), or cook a gourmet meal. These are all relatively normal things that present a certain amount of risk. What if the person of the opposite sex doesn't respond positively to your flirtation? What if you do not lose weight or increase your athleticism, despite starting a new fitness routine? What if you burn all the food in the pan for your gourmet meal?

These are all legitimate concerns, and I go through the same self-questioning when I undertake something new in life. The key, though, is realizing the simple answer to these questions: *"It does not matter if I fail. I will simply pick myself back up and try again."*

It can be scary investing money in a business, talking to a member of the opposite sex, starting a workout plan, or cooking a gourmet meal. You can 100% avoid failure, too, if you simply never try any of these things. But I can guarantee you the not-trying strategy will leave you feeling entirely unfulfilled and left out of many good things in life. This is actually a much bigger failure, and you will realize it as you watch other people around you continuing to succeed after taking risks. Sure, they will strike out from time to time, but those home runs you see them hitting are only possible because they swung the bat.

Personally, I know for a fact I never would have generated the money I made on Craigslist had I waited for the "right moment," when I felt totally comfortable in a given purchasing or selling situation.

Bottom line, you will never know what you are made of unless you take a swing or two, or three, or ten, or a hundred. Yes, it might take quite a few tries to "get it right" with something in life, but it is all worth it in the end. The sooner you start swinging the bat, the sooner you will get there.

CHAPTER 7 RECAP

- Take confident action to capture the benefit of existing opportunities.
- *Risk = Reward.* Great rewards are almost never realized without some risk.
- Err on the side of taking action when you are on the verge, but not totally decided.
- Regularly put yourself out of your comfort zone to learn where "Intelligent Decision-Making" blends optimally with "Risk-Taking Mentality."

Taking action is much easier said than done, so it is very important that you internalize the importance of taking action to give yourself sufficient motivation to actually *do* it. Do not look at this chapter as just another silly motivational speech that gives mere lip service to making things happen in life. Take it seriously and apply it. It will bring you significant benefits in all your business and personal endeavors.

Assignments

1. Take one step towards building your Craigslist business, even something as simple as browsing current listings, immediately upon completion of this chapter. The purpose of this is to reinforce the need to take action. Taking action right now reinforces the need to stay committed to your goals in the short term and the long term and prevents you from putting off the things you need to do to arrive at the finish line.

2. Take a risk in another area of your life, outside of Craigslist. Whether it is trying a yoga class, cooking a gourmet meal, asking out that special someone, or singing in public – come up with something that gives you pause, then power through

it to the end. Regardless of the outcome, you will feel empowered by confidently executing your plan.

<u>On Deck</u>

In the next chapter, we will review the competitive advantages to be gained by being prompt. In contrast with being late or behind the eight ball, being prompt carries two related meanings that are both important in the execution of successful deals.

8

BE PROMPT

TWO POWERFUL REASONS TO BE ON TIME

This chapter covers two related but independent concepts when it comes to being prompt: Punctuality and Opportunism. Combining these forces can amount to a powerhouse of business acumen when harnessed properly.

Preparation
Planning & Measuring
Deal Analysis
Purchasing
Sales

Punctuality is a simple matter of being on time, and is a basic prerequisite for professional success. It builds trust and reliability over time, too.

Opportunism is recognizing a great business deal and capitalizing on it before others do. It can mean the difference between cashing in on a huge deal and missing it altogether.

When someone combines consistent punctuality with intelligent opportunism, we can say that person is both sharp and poised. This gives you an edge that will help you convert more deals and get "lucky" more often. In reality, luck is often a function of consistently putting yourself in the right place at the right time.

1. Punctuality

Punctuality is a universal measure of both competence and success in the professional world. Being early, or at least being on time, goes a long way towards establishing your credibility and showing others that you care about them and respect their time. You will not receive any extra credit from others for being on time, though, and you should not expect to, since it is a basic duty.

However, you will certainly be docked plenty of points each time you are late. This may even happen without your knowledge, as your boss, peers, clients, and vendors silently draw conclusions about your capacity for responsibility. Instead of being known as reliable and dependable, you could be labeled a disorganized flake. Ouch.

Believe it or not, I used to be one of these disorganized flakes myself. If you are anything like the old me, it may be unusual for you to be on time to anything at all! But not to worry; later in this chapter I will teach you an effective strategy for being on time. You will soon come to see yourself as a finely tuned machine, always on time and ready for business. You will trust yourself more as you tally up mark after mark of punctuality, and this will cause others to shift their perception of you in a positive way.

By the way, do understand that it takes time to establish trust and credibility if you have been late most of your life. Be patient with yourself and others, then, while you work on this part of your life. Luckily, it only takes a few weeks to nail down a new habit, and only a few months after that to establish reliability and dependability in the eyes of others.

Now let's look more in depth at what it means to be "punctual" on Craigslist.

Punctuality in Initial Correspondence

Punctuality on Craigslist starts with the initial correspondence that occurs before the actual in-person meeting. Being prompt with emails and phone calls shows professionalism and gives you more credibility in the eyes of the other party working on a transaction with you. The other person will be more likely to follow through on a deal with you because of your perceived attentiveness and ability to follow through. This in turn leads to a higher "conversion rate" in terms of successful sales after initiating communication with potential buyers (or purchases after initiating communication with sellers).

Plain and simple, prompt and sure communication shows the world that you are interested, attentive, reliable, and ready for business. It is a sign that you will follow through on your end of the bargain when it comes time to meet, too. Nobody likes dealing with someone who is flaky, takes forever to respond, and is generally unpredictable or poor at communicating when doing business of any kind. I have found this to be true in every one of my many business circles and personal groups. There is so much to be gained by being punctual, timely, and promptly communicative with the people you work with and rely on every day.

Punctuality in Email and Phone Communications

As a general rule, you should never go longer than 24-48 hours between communications on Craigslist, and preferably, you will communicate even more frequently than this. I believe a more functional level of punctuality and follow-up is no more than 4-6 hours between emails or phone calls. I do this to ensure I do not lose precious time or risk someone else getting involved in a deal I could otherwise close by being quick about it.

I know this may sound demanding. It may seem like it requires a lot of your attention. The truth is, it does – unless you have a smartphone, which can simply beep at you when you need to pay attention.

You must pay constant attention and keep your head in the game if you want to succeed. I have lost good deals by forgetting to call people back or not emailing them in a timely manner, leaving them to work out a deal with someone else by the time I finally came around. In some cases, waiting "too long" was only a matter of hours.

Understand that Craigslist, and business in general, is not a walk in the park; it is more like being in the flow of traffic on a busy road. You must be alert, pay attention, and stay focused at all times. There is a common "speed" to things, and just as cars on the road are expected to drive somewhere at or above the speed limit, so too the deal-makers in business will be accelerating and driving forward with their plans and communications at a certain rate.

The good news is that being attentive to your communications does not require a large quantity of *time*. Notice the difference between attention and time. Attention is simply being able to mentally loop back around to something at a particular point in time. Time is, well, time. I frequently notice people confusing these two things, though, thinking that it will take "all kinds of time" to *pay attention* to something. In reality, it only requires a little training, and the advent of smart phones has made it all really quite simple.

Paying attention can be automated on your smartphone by setting alarms, appointments, and reminders. On the execution side of things, your emails, texts, and phone calls can all be shot back and forth in minutes. Also, most phones will notify you when you receive new emails, texts, and calls. All of this in one device. Amazing, I know.

The bottom line is that you should aim for same-day follow-up in all of your Craigslist endeavors. This is because Craigslist transactions tend to go very quickly once a buyer and seller connect, and should the communication die out, often the deal dies out with it.

By the way, I have discovered that email conversations on Craigslist and similar mediums tend to go back and forth at least a few times before a deal is reached or dismissed. On the other hand, phone calls tend to settle issues right away. Emails are still okay, and in fact, I actually rely on them most of the time because they are both easy and passive. When I really want to hammer home a deal, though, I will get on the phone and talk it through.

Whether you arrive at an agreed-upon deal via phone or email, the next natural step is to schedule a meeting time and place. My typical strategy for this part of the process is to suggest one or two times that work for me at the location of my choosing. We will discuss location control more in Chapter 11, but for now we can stay focused on the importance of being on time, regardless of where the meeting is scheduled.

Being On Time to Meetings

When showing up to meetings resulting from Craigslist interactions, you want to be on time for the sake of your reputation and for the sake of the deal at hand. When you show up late, you risk the other person bailing out of the deal prior to your arrival. Moreover, the other person might turn out to be someone you would like to befriend or network with, but now you are starting your relationship with them after a first impression of tardiness. The importance of first impressions really cannot be overstated.

You might be inclined to think it does not matter whether or not you are on time with Craigslist deals. You may figure that you will never see the other person again, or that they will likely be late, too. These things might be true from time to time, but making such assumptions is a cup-half-empty way to look at life. It is not the correct mindset to be in.

Instead, you want to constantly be on the lookout for new

opportunities, whether they be resale opportunities, relationships, or other great things. The cup needs to be half-full; you need to be prepared for success and greatness to strike at any time. You never know when you will run into a life-changing opportunity, or even a very small but worthwhile opportunity, and if you are not prepared for it, then you have sold yourself short.

Personally, I have run into quite a few people a second or third time after meeting them through Craigslist, and in some cases, I showed up to a meeting only to discover the other person was someone I had met through another channel in the past. I have also gone on to do larger-scale business with some of the folks I have met through Craigslist, and who knows whether or not they would have trusted my abilities if I had not taken our original meeting Craigslist seriously. Fortunately for me, I protected my reputation from such pitfalls ahead of time by maintaining punctuality and professionalism.

For those of you out there who still scoff at the idea of being perfectly on time to a simple Craigslist meeting, let me remind you that I used to be just like you. Never in my wildest dreams did I think it would be possible that I would make a legitimate friend through a Craigslist transaction or go on to do bigger business with that person elsewhere. But at some point, I shifted my mindset, and that is just when those cool things started to happen. Life has this funny way of manifesting the things that we dwell on, for better or for worse.

Learn Punctuality by Getting Up On Time

The following self-improvement tip is borrowed with the gracious permission of Steve Pavlina atwww.stevepavlina.com. According to his copyright release, all the work on his site is in the public domain and available for commercial use. The release is located here:

http://www.stevepavlina.com/blog/2010/12/releasing-my-copyrights/

Thanks, Steve.

The tool he discusses in this article has to do with using subconscious programming to wake up on time in the morning -- as in first thing, when the alarm goes off. His promise is that, with this exercise, you will not be tempted to snooze or sleep through another alarm again, and I can testify to the accuracy of this myself, having done the exercise. Though I *do* like sleeping in on the weekends when I can!

The reason this is such a powerful exercise is because the core tool used (subconscious programming) can be exploited for other purposes. Learning to wake up right away when your alarm goes off is a big enough deal in itself, but once you achieve that, you can move onto programming your mind and body to do all sorts of other things. Now, let's see what Steve has to say about waking up on time.

Steve Pavlina's Article on Waking Up on Time

When your alarm wakes you up in the morning, is it hard for you to get up right away? Do you find yourself hitting the snooze button and going right back to sleep?

That used to be part of my daily awakening ritual too. When my alarm would blare its infernal noise, I'd turn the damned thing off right away. Then under the cloak of that early morning brain fog, I'd slowly ponder whether or not I should actually get up:

It's nice and warm under the covers. If I get up, it's going to be cold. That won't be too pleasant.

Oh, I really should get up now. C'mon legs... move. Go, legs, go. Hmmm... that isn't how I move my legs, is it? They don't seem to be listening to me.

I should go to the gym. Yeah. Hmmm... I don't really feel like working out right now though. I haven't even had breakfast. Maybe I should have a muffin first. Banana nut. Now that's a good muffin.

Maybe I'm trying to get myself up too early. I'm still sleepy, aren't I? Maybe getting up with an alarm is unnatural. Won't I function better with more sleep?

I don't have to get up right this minute, do I? Surely I can relax another five minutes or so. The world isn't going to end if I don't get up right now.

[Scootch... scootch... Zzzzzzzz]

Two hours later...

Me: What time is it? I don't even remember the alarm going off. Oh well, guess I'll have to skip exercise today.

Fast forward to present day...

My alarm goes off sometime between 4:00 and 5:00am... never later than 5:00am, even on weekends and holidays. I turn off the alarm within a few seconds. My lungs inflate with a deep breath of air, and I stretch my limbs out in all directions for about two seconds. Soon my feet hit the floor, and I find myself getting dressed while my wife snoozes on. I go downstairs to grab a piece of fruit, pop into my home office to catch up on some emails, and then it's off to the gym at 5:15.

But this time there's no voice inside my head debating what I should do. It's not even a positive voice this time — it's just not there. The whole thing happens on autopilot, even before I feel fully awake mentally. I can't say it requires any self-discipline to do this every morning because it's a totally conditioned response. It's like my conscious mind is just along for the ride while my subconscious controls my body. When my alarm goes off each morning, I respond just like Pavlov's dogs. It would actually be harder for me not to get up when my alarm goes off.

So how do you go from scenario one to scenario two?

First, let's consider the way most people tackle this problem — what I consider the wrong way.

The wrong way is to try using your conscious willpower to get yourself out of bed each morning. That might work every once in a while, but let's face it — you're not always going to be thinking straight the moment your alarm goes off. You may experience what I call the fog of brain. The decisions you make in that state won't necessarily be the ones you'd make when you're fully conscious and alert. You can't really trust yourself... nor should you.

If you use this approach, you're likely to fall into a trap. You decide to get up at a certain time in advance, but then you undo that decision when the alarm goes off. At 10pm you decide it would be a good idea to get up at 5am. But at 5am you decide it would be a better idea to get up at 8am. But let's face it — you know the 10pm decision is the one you really want implemented... if only you could get your 5am self to go along with it.

Now some people, upon encountering this conundrum, will conclude that they simply need more discipline. And that's actually somewhat true, but not in the way you'd expect. If you want to get up at 5am, you don't need more discipline at 5am. You don't need better self-talk. You don't need two or three alarm clocks scattered around the room. And you don't need an advanced alarm that includes technology from NASA's astronaut toilets.

You actually need more discipline when you're fully awake and conscious: the discipline to know that you can't trust yourself to make intelligent, conscious decisions the moment you first wake up. You need the discipline to accept that you're not going to make the right call at 5am. Your 5am coach is no good, so you need to fire him.

What's the real solution then? The solution is to delegate the problem. Turn the whole thing over to your subconscious mind. Cut your conscious mind out of the loop.

Now how do you do this? The same way you learned any other repeatable skill. You practice until it becomes rote. Eventually your subconscious will take over and run the script on autopilot.

This is going to sound really stupid, but it works. Practice getting up as soon as your alarm goes off. That's right — practice. But don't do it in the morning. Do it during the day when you're wide awake.

Go to your bedroom, and set the room conditions to match your desired wake-up time as best you can. Darken the room, or practice in the evening just after sunset so it's already dark. If you sleep in pajamas, put on your pajamas. If you brush your teeth before bed, then brush your teeth. If you take off your glasses or contacts when you sleep, then take those off too.

Set your alarm for a few minutes ahead. Lie down in bed just like you would if you were sleeping, and close your eyes. Get into your favorite sleep position. Imagine it's early in the morning... a few minutes before your desired wake-up time. Pretend you're actually asleep. Visualize a dream location, or just zone out as best you can.

Now when your alarm goes off, turn it off as fast as you can. Then take a deep breath to fully inflate your lungs, and stretch your limbs out in all directions for a couple seconds... like you're stretching during a yawn. Then sit up, plant your feet on the floor, and stand up. Smile a big smile. Then proceed to do the very next action you'd like to do upon waking. For me it's getting dressed.

Now shake yourself off, restore the pre-waking conditions, return to bed, reset your alarm, and repeat. Do this over and over and over until it becomes so automatic that you run through the whole ritual without thinking about it. If you have to sub vocalize any of the steps (i.e. if you hear a mental voice coaching you on what to do), you're not there yet.

Feel free to devote several sessions over a period of days to this practice. Think of it like doing sets and reps at the gym. Do one or two sets per day at different times... and perhaps 3-10 reps each time.

Yes, it will take some time to do this, but that time is nothing compared to how much time you'll save in the long run. A few hours of practice today can save you hundreds of hours each year.

With enough practice — I can't give you an accurate estimate of how long it will take because it will be different for everyone – you'll condition a new physiological response to the sound of your alarm. When your alarm goes off, you'll get up automatically without even thinking about it. The more you run the pattern, the stronger it will become. Eventually it will be uncomfortable not to get up when your alarm goes off. It will feel like putting on your pants with the opposite leg first.

You can also practice mentally if you're good at visualizing. Mental practice is faster, but I think it's best to run through the whole thing physically. There are subtle details you might miss if you only rehearse mentally, and you want your subconscious to capture the real flavor of the experience. So if you do use mental practice, at least do it physically the first few times.

The more you practice your wake-up ritual, the deeper you'll ingrain this habit into your subconscious. Alarm goes off -> get up immediately. Alarm goes off -> get up immediately. Alarm goes off -> get up immediately.

Once this becomes a daily habit, you won't have to do anymore daytime practice. This type of habit is self-reinforcing. You only have to go through the conditioning period once. Then you're basically set for life until you decide to change it. Even if you fall out of the habit for some reason (like an extended vacation in a different time zone), you'll be able to return to it more easily. Think of it like muscle memory. Once you've grooved in the pattern, it will still be there even if you let some weeds grow over it.

Any behavior pattern you experience when your alarm goes off will become self-reinforcing if you repeat it enough times. Chances are that you already have a well-established wake-up ritual, but it may not be the one you want. The more you repeat your existing pattern, the more you condition it into your subconscious. Every time you fail to get up when your alarm goes off, that becomes ever more your default physiological response. If you want to change that behavior, you'll need to undertake a conscious reconditioning program such as the one I described above.

Beating yourself up about your bad wake-up habits will not work — in fact, you'll just condition these mental beatings as part of the very routine you're trying to change. Not only will you not get up when your alarm goes off, but you'll also automatically beat yourself up about it. How lame is that? Do you really want to keep running that dumb pattern for the rest of your life? That's exactly what will happen if you don't condition a more empowering pattern. For good or ill, your habits will make or break you.

Once you establish your desired wake-up ritual, I recommend you stick with it every single day – 7 days a week, 365 days a year. And for the first 30 days, set your alarm for the same time every day. Once the habit is established, then you can vary your wake-up times or occasionally go without the alarm if you want to sleep in, but until then it's best to keep the pattern very tight. That way it will become your default behavior, and you'll be able to stray from time to time without serious risk of deconditioning it.

I'm confident that once you establish this habit, you'll absolutely love it. I consider this to be one my most productive habits. It saves me hundreds of hours a year, and it keeps paying dividends day after day. I also found this habit extremely valuable during my polyphasic sleep experiment.

Think about it — if you oversleep just 30 minutes a day, that's 180+ hours a year. And if you're at 60 minutes a day, that's 365 hours a year, the equivalent of nine 40-hour weeks. That's a lot of time! Now I don't know about you, but I can think of more creative things to do with that time than lying in bed longer than I need to.

I encourage you to give this method a try. I know it seems silly to practice getting out of bed, but hey, what if it works? What if you knew with total certainty that if you set your alarm for a certain time, you would absolutely get up at that time no matter what? There's no reason you can't create that for yourself over the next few days. Practice makes permanent.

Applications of This Strategy

Like I mentioned before this excerpt, the core principle of subconscious programming can be used to condition a variety of responses. Whenever there are certain situations we want to handle in a different way, we can condition our new responses quite literally by physically and mentally practicing the response we wish to have.

When it comes to punctuality, all you need to do is set two alarms and then condition your responses appropriately. The first alarm is a preparation alarm. It should be set a certain amount of time before the event takes place, which allows you to undertake any necessary preparation before actually leaving. For instance, if your goal is to arrive at work on time in the morning, you should calculate how long it actually takes to get ready after you get up, then add in five minutes as a margin of error.

The second alarm is for when you leave. It should be set about two minutes prior to when you actually need to walk out the door. This alarm alerts you that it is time to wrap up the current activity, end any conversations, grab your things, pick up your keys, and walk out the door. Another margin of error should already be built in to account for traffic and variations in transit time.

That way, even on a day when you are tired, the dog is constipated, *and* you hit traffic, you still stand a good chance of arriving on time. Instead of making excuses about traffic, the dog, or having to admit to your boss that you slept in, you get to avoid all of that and move on confidently with your day. Not to mention that, on most days, all of these delays will not happen at the same time, and you will wind up being a little early.

You may think arriving early to something means you will be twiddling your thumbs for 5-10 minutes or more while you wait for everyone else to arrive. I used to think this way myself, but speaking from experience, this will not be the case most of the time. If it does happen, though, that you are either a bit early or the other person is a bit late, use those few minutes in a productive way.

Catch up on your voicemails. Check out some new Craigslist listings. Respond to pending emails, read a news article or book, or relax with your eyes closed for a few minutes. Maybe even do some positive visualization work while sitting in your car. Bottom line: you should stay committed to being on time and simply take advantage of short breaks to get ahead on other things.

Now that I have given you the tools to be a powerhouse of punctuality and prompt communications, we can move onto the next section: *Opportunism.*

2. Opportunism

Being opportunistic is fairly simple; you just need to cultivate some ambition and decision-making skills. On Craigslist, this means you must stay up-to-date on current listings, know what certain products tend to sell for (see Chapter 6), and then take *prompt* action when you see those products listed at the lower end of the price range you've previously researched and determined you will buy in.

In a nutshell, opportunism is a two-step process:

1) Identify an opportunity
2) Capitalize *promptly* on the opportunity

In the last chapter, I told a story about breaking my own rules (by driving a far distance) to purchase an accordion for resale. Plain and simple, I knew I had to jump on it before anyone else had a chance to buy it. Recognizing a potentially sizeable deal, I knew I had to act before the opportunity passed.

This is how you must operate on a minute-to-minute basis: quickly and with adequate risk tolerance. This is what opportunism is all about. You will never have all the information you need to feel absolutely sure of any given situation, so you must get comfortable making decisions under uncertainty.

U.S. Marine Training

U.S. Marines are trained in a specific manner to make prompt, confident decisions under uncertainty. They are trained this way because hundreds of years of military research, statistics, and historical data have shown that military leaders who make prompt, intelligent decisions come out on top.

Specifically, the Marines have identified that it is better to make a series of prompt, reasonably calculated decisions with an imperfect success rate than to risk losing the initiative. Losing the initiative is what happens when we hesitate, hem and haw, or otherwise fail to take action.

In the *Marine Corps Gazette* (May, 1999), General Charles C. Krulak explains how Marines must rapidly distinguish between useful information and that which does not apply. In particular, he points out they must abstain from delaying their decision until more information makes the situation clearer, lest they lose the initiative. As he puts it, "In all likelihood, once military action is underway, more information will simply further cloud the picture. Our leaders must be able to "feel" the battlefield tempo, discern patterns among the chaos, and make decisions in seconds ... much like a Wall Street investment trader, but with life threatening consequences."

He then goes on to discuss the difference between two very different models of decision-making: the analytical model and the intuitive, recognitional model.

In summary, the analytical model is based on the evaluation of *quantitative* options, and its success depends on having a relatively high degree of certainty about the circumstances at hand. By contrast, the intuitive or recognitional model relies on the decider's experience, judgment, and ultimately, a *qualitative* situational assessment. Rather than attempting to identify an ideal solution, the decider's goal is to identify and proceed with the first solution that will work.

The analytical model offers certain advantages when there is ample time to thoroughly explore, measure, and analyze a fair quantity of pertinent information. However, absence such circumstances, it has been shown that the recognitional model is better since its focus is on functionality, rather than perfection.

General Krulak shares an interesting point regarding the frequency at which we use each of these two models. "Research by noted psychologist Dr. Gary Klein indicates that most people use the recognitional, or intuitive, model of decision-making over 90 percent of the time."However, he goes on to explain how most of us will switch to the analytical model of thinking when confronted by *new situations* in which we do not have much experience, or which seem particularly *stressful or intimidating*, and our tendency is to delay/stall until more information becomes available.

If you ever notice yourself switching to the analytical model of decision-making in such a situation, remind yourself that you are missing opportunities by delaying your decision, then refocus your energy on intuitive resources and quickly decide how to proceed.

It is funny how opportunities in life can so easily pass us by if we are not ready for them. It might be a phone call from an important client that we do not pick up, a major life decision we are not ready to make, an attractive member of the opposite sex who leaves the room while we hesitate, or an item for resale that we do not buy when the price is right. When things seem like a big deal, it is easy for us to freeze and avoid taking action.

Strangely enough, though, even if our approach is less than perfect, a sizeable percentage of the time we will achieve our objective by taking simple, decisive steps to get there. Whether this means picking up the phone before it goes to voicemail, confidently making a difficult life decision and truly owning it, introducing yourself to that cute member of the opposite sex without delay, or purchasing an item for resale when the price seems good, we can succeed a good amount of the time by getting out of our head and just *doing* these things. Like Nike says, *Just Do It!*

Making decisions quickly does mean that we will experience the occasional failure. But you already know this is to be embraced, as periodic failures are inevitable on the road to long-term success. Marine officers fail, too, but they do so confidently as the result of prompt decision-making. They know temporary failures represent progress and are a positive marker that action has been taken towards their goal. Then they recover quickly and get back to action. By adopting the same attitude, you can move yourself closer to your goals than ever before.

Bringing Decision-Making Back Into Focus

As you start reviewing Craigslist listings on a more regular basis, you will begin to notice the occasional listing priced just below market value. This represents an opportunity to be immediately capitalized on, as you have realized it is already priced on the low side of things.

However, even if you do not "know" for a fact that the item in question is absolutely priced below market value, I urge you to trust your gut if it *feels* like it is priced below market value.

Sometimes, like with my organ and accordion acquisitions, this will be the case. Something will just hit you in the gut and tell you to take action. It is like having a big "aha!" moment. You can still do some cursory research to validate your feelings, but ultimately, you will want to get in touch with the seller as soon as possible. Otherwise, another savvy buyer might snatch up the opportunity before you can capitalize on it.

Of course, the lower someone lists a product, the faster it will sell (which should make sense due to the laws of supply and demand!). This is why it is so important to get right on the phone and/or email when you notice such listings. In fact, in some cases, you will even hear of buyers making offers *higher* than the listed price to "reserve" the item until they can arrive to purchase it, if they feel the deal is so good that they might be threatened by other buyers.

What about situations where there are products listed on the lower side of market value, but not really low enough to turn a profit? In these situations, you can make an offer that is lower than the listing price. The seller is not obliged to accept your offer, but you might as well try. Note that we first discussed this at the end of Chapter 6.

This is truly one of my go-to methods for drumming up new inventory at the right price. When there are no obvious "deals" available, I contact lots of sellers and make lots of offers, even though only a certain percentage of sellers will accept them. As we learned in Chapter 1, this principle is called the "Law of Averages." I am attempting to manufacture deals where they do not currently exist, and I am successful a good amount of the time.

However, you should know that I avoid making offers that are substantially lower than someone's asking price. Offering someone considerably less than what they are asking, for example 50% of their listing price, is only going to be a waste of time for everybody – even if the seller has his or her item listed 200% higher than it should be. Most people are willing to haggle a little bit, but not that much.

My basic rule of thumb is to offer at least 70% of the person's asking price. Of course, the lower you go, the better the deal will be for you if the other party agrees. However, if the seller is receiving offers from other buyers, you also must consider the fact that someone else might submit a better offer right after yours.

Let's Drill It In

Let me repeat one more time: *Prompt, decisive action must be taken to catalyze success.*

In my opinion, this may be the most difficult part of this book to understand and apply, but please stick with it, give yourself a chance, and commit to becoming the type of person who confidently and comfortably takes decisive action amidst uncertainty.

I have faith in you and every reason to believe that you have what it takes – we all do – it's just a matter of getting started and keeping up with it. Do this and I absolutely promise you it will pay dividends in every area of your life, especially in your Craigslist deals and other business endeavors.

CHAPTER 8 RECAP

- Get lucky by combining punctuality with opportunism.
- Use punctuality to maintain professionalism, trust, and reliability.
- Program punctuality into your subconscious and manage it with alarms.
- Identify great deals and opportunities.
- Take prompt, decisive action.

There are two key lessons in this chapter: *Punctuality* and *Opportunism*. Both of them play into what I call being the "Early Bird." Consistent punctuality will turn you into a powerhouse of professionalism and reliability. Opportunism will bring you more opportunities and a greater ability to profit from them. As you get comfortable taking prompt action on a regular basis, you will also gain confidence from being able to put yourself on the line, regardless of the outcome. This confidence will translate into success when applied to your business dealings.

Assignments

1. Punctuality: Use Steve Pavlina's method of subconscious programming to train yourself to respond to alarms. Whether you use his method to train yourself to wake up on time, leave the house on time, or in some other way, put it into action TODAY and get the training/programming started. Within the next two weeks, I want you showing up on time to work and to your business and personal appointments.

2. Continue browsing the listings in your area of focus on Craigslist to internalize more information about prices. This will ultimately help you identify and leverage the many "ripe fruit" opportunities that exist in your local market.

On Deck

In the next chapter, we will focus on the importance of "playing nice" with others. More specifically, we will discuss how to see your transactions as win-win situations instead of zero-sum games, build friends out of your business contacts, and stay positive and professional in your communications with others.

9

PLAY NICE

LEVERAGING EMOTIONAL INTELLIGENCE FOR GREATER RESULTS

The purpose of this chapter is to discuss the value of "playing nice," or more simply put, adopting a positive outlook towards the folks you meet on Craigslist.

Preparation
Planning & Measuring
Deal Analysis
Purchasing
Sales

There is a measurable value to being positive, professional, helpful, and friendly with others in both business and personal life. It is no secret that people want to do business with people they like; you can verify this for yourself by considering whether or not you would want to do business with someone you do *not* like very much.

Before we get knee-deep in the relationship-building stuff, though, let me give you an insight on how I approach this part of my business on Craigslist. Try to keep this in mind as you move forward with this book, because I feel it is an important part of what keeps the flame alive for me.

Behind the business component of my Craigslist transactions, there is another purpose for me that transcends the financial: my desire to try new things, expand my knowledge in my niche, meet other people with similar interests, make new friends, and up cycle (repurpose and/or improve the condition of) used gear in need of repair or rejuvenation. For instance, whenever I pick up a guitar and have my tech fix the intonation, put on new strings, and polish it up, it makes me feel good to know I am leaving the instrument better than I found it.

Having a deeper purpose like this is important. It provides meaningful motivation and drive beyond the money, and it leads to a deeper sense of fulfillment. It can also lead to more real connections with the folks you meet, and better karma with them as you engage in deals. Because of this, I would recommend that you pick an area of interest for your deals that will provide a similar sense of fulfillment and sharing with others. You will have more in common with the people you meet and more easily build relationships with them.

This brings us back to the main point. You must always try to build positive relationships with other people, especially in business. Make connections and *learn to see others as allies*, not as enemies. Even if Craigslist *is* a transactional marketplace where you are unlikely to see most of the people you meet more than once, try to see the positive benefit in meeting and knowing more people. Get into a mindset of abundance before stepping into your interpersonal communications with others. This sets you up for success, draws people in, helps you close deals, and allows you to make new friends and business contacts.

Besides, your own success actually *depends* on your ability to get along with people. When you are focused on being professional, upbeat, and friendly, it is easier to engage in a meaningful conversation with them, build that relationship, and ultimately get what you want from the interaction— whether that's a purchase or a sale.

This is a Win-Win Game

Too many people see Craigslist deals (and perhaps life in general) as a zero-sum game: somebody wins, somebody loses. You better not be the loser, so you have to win at all costs, right? Wrong.

You *have* to see business dealings as *win-win* situations, where all parties stand to gain. Part of this stems from a paradigm of creating and delivering value when purchasing items for resale. This applies not only to Craigslist, but to all types of business.

As a seller, for me this often means getting to know the buyer, asking them questions about their background, asking what they plan to do with the item I am selling them, and so on. This is especially true with buyers who are on the fence about making a purchase, new to the industry, or are buying for someone else (like a family member or friend).

With these types of buyers, if I truly do not feel they stand to benefit from what I am selling, I will be brutally honest with them about it. It might sound silly, but I have talked several buyers out of large deals that would have been very good for me, simply because I knew it was not good for them. It's always best to do right by people, build up a bank of positive karma, and solidify your reputation in a positive manner.

Do Not Concern Yourself with a Particular Sale

I am truly not worried about making or losing any given sale. It's easy for a novice salesperson to get emotionally attached to a potential sale once the buyer has expressed some interest, and get caught up (emotionally) in "closing" the sale – to the point that they can't see the big picture anymore, forgetting that no one sale really matters in the long run. Getting lost in this sort of tunnel vision can be destructive in many ways, and can take one's focus away from the things that really matter.

Instead, I *am* worried about cultivating positive relationships with people. In order to build and maintain those relationships, the sale must be secondary. Priority must be given to the other person's goals and interests. How can I help them reach a goal or solve a problem they are facing? What is it they want to accomplish with the thing I have to offer them?

If they are the seller, do they need money to fund some other purchase or transfer value into a different part of their life? Are they just looking for a trade? If they are the buyer, what are their reasons for desiring the item I have for sale, and how can it really help them?

When I am the seller, if I recognize that someone does not really want or need something they are about to buy from me, I will let them know why I think they might be barking up the wrong tree.

Besides, I may have alternative items for sale that *are* a better fit for them. I have sold a few things this way, and not only does it make me feel good to steer them in the right direction, it makes them feel good about their resulting purchase. In some cases, these alternatives were more expensive, and in other cases, they were less expensive. The price is beside the point.

By providing my expertise to folks in this fashion, I am creating and delivering value beyond what would normally be expected in a Craigslist transaction. I believe this is the right thing to do, and I enjoy making friends in the local music community in the process.

Treating Others Well Pays Off

I cannot tell you how times I have completed a deal and had it lead to future business down the road, or even a new friend. Some folks I have met through Craigslist have also gone on to do business with me in my other businesses, which is a huge win in itself.

For example, here is a screenshot of the ad I placed for my BC Rich Warlock bass guitar, sans the pictures I had posted at the time:

BC Rich Warlock Bass Guitar - $150 (Greater SD Area)

BC Rich Warlock bass. Great pickup combination, comes with locking/rotating strap. Strings haven't been changed for a while and some of the knobs are a little wonky, but 100% functional and sounds awesome. I've recorded studio tracks with this exact bass in the past and it sounds big and mean in the lows. Gigged live at the Belly Up in the past few months, sounded awesome.

$150 OBO / trades OK too

These are $300 new on musicians friend, $192 used. 4.3 / 5 stars based on 71 reviews. http://www.musiciansfriend.com/bass/b.c.-rich-bronze-warlock-electric-bass-guitar

The picture is a shot of the actual item for sale, taken on 3/1/13.

After a few weeks, I found a buyer, and when it came time to do the deal, I had him meet me at my workplace for the sake of convenience. As it turned out, he was in need of the services I provide at my primary workplace, and several months later, he got back in touch to request a sales quote. We ended up doing business together again, this time through my primary workplace.

I have also done deals with people who have gone on to do business with some of my friends, and because of their past connection with me, there was common ground that created a friendlier environment to do so. You get the point.

This is where you want to end up, too, and all it takes is a halfway positive attitude and a willingness to be open to others. It really counts to treat others the way you would like to be treated. Speaking of which, we will cover specific ways to make others "feel" heard and listened to in Chapter 12, when we discuss negotiation.

Avoid Negativity; Stay Focused on the Positive

Sometimes, even with the best of intentions, if you have a short temper, you may need to put some real effort into holding yourself in check when you encounter someone negative. There are all kinds of people out there, and some of them exist for the sole purpose of driving you and me nuts. It is no surprise that a good portion of these folks are on Craigslist.

THEY WILL SEND YOU EMAILS IN ALL CAPITAL LETTERS LIKE THEY ARE YELLING AT YOU and you will not know why. Others will personally attack you for seemingly no reason, or they will get upset about something in your listing or your offer.

I know this because I deal with it all the time. *All* the time, and often out of the blue. Take this guy, for example, who seeks nothing more than to pick a fight over something extremely petty:

To: njfrb-4245042687@sale.craigslist.org
Sent: Saturday, January 4, 2014 9:10 PM
Subject: Les Paul Standard, Beautiful Gold Top

That is NOT a gold top.
You should think about how misleading people will likely HURT your chances of selling this POS. I have seen this guitar up here a while ago, and you wonder why.
Market it appropriately, and enjoy the sale.

Unthankfully

Ricky W.

This is a perfect example of someone you should ignore. Ricky is not interested in purchasing my guitar, and frankly, I am not really sure what his agenda is. Apparently, I have incorrectly listed the color of the guitar, which to him was extremely misleading, even though I provided eight photos clearly showing all the details of the instrument.

How should you handle this type of situation? Easy – delete the email and ignore it altogether. This type of correspondence simply does not warrant a response.

You might be tempted to fire an argumentative or negative email back to someone like this, but it would not be productive. It would likely provoke a lengthy and hostile exchange with the other person, and serve no meaningful purpose (except, perhaps, to increase your blood pressure and rob you of your precious time). At the end of the day, as frustrating as it can be to deal with folks like this, it's not your job to set every jerk in the world straight. Plus, you never know who you might end up meeting or seeing again down the line.

Realize: _Little distractions like this can eat away at you, suck away_ _your time, drain you of emotion and energy, cause you to dwell on_ _negative interactions, and turn you off to doing business on_ _Craigslist or through other online trading mediums._

However, this is only possible _if_ you let the negative distractions get the better of you. When you are tough and let it slide off your back without a second thought, you have instantly freed yourself to focus on what matters.

In the very few disputes I have had with folks on Craigslist, most were your standard email disputes, where people say things they would not have the _cajones_ to say face-to-face.

It bothers me that I remember these few disputes, too. The only reason I can remember them is because I chose to let myself go there with them in the first place. On the other hand, in all the times I ignored potential disputes and simply walked the other way, it was a huge relief. I did not have to dwell on anything or anyone, because I never really let it into my mind in the first place. This is where you want to be: calm, collected, and unaffected by conflict.

Remind yourself that you have better things to do with your time than give your attention to useless, negative distractions. This is true whether they come in the form of things, people, or both. Stay in control. Use the NLP trick from Chapter 2, if you need to, to reset your mind and mood. In the time you waste sending a flame email back to someone who was rude to you, you could have scanned two pages of listings and emailed an offer on your next deal.

Doing the Right Thing

While we are discussing relationship building, there is one more subject I should briefly touch on. Part of treating people correctly and forming positive relationships is maintaining good business ethics. I think most of us already know this and operate this way by default. Following the Golden Rule and treating people the way we would like to be treated goes a long way. It is something that can help you establish real trust and meaningful relationships in both business and personal life.

In Conclusion

Having a positive attitude and well-intended interactions is integral to my system, and I stand strongly behind this. Not to mention, karma really does matter.

As the world gets bigger, so too does it get smaller, and I continue to be surprised by how many folks I run into that I met sometime in the past. Some from deals, some from a past job, some from school... they are everywhere, and they all carry some knowledge and opinion of me. By leaving these people with good vibes, I set myself up for future success if and when I run into them again.

CHAPTER 9 RECAP

- Develop a deeper purpose for your business transactions for maximum fulfillment.
- Take a win-win perspective on completing your deals.
- Be more concerned with relationship building than individual transactions.
- Stay focused on the positive and avoid wasting time on negative distractions.
- Always treat others properly – it pays off in the end.

This chapter is a primer on managing relationships in business. The crux of it is that building good relationships is fundamental to doing good business, because other people's decisions are influenced by their feelings about you. If you show them respect and care about their needs, they will reflect this back to you and be more eager to build a business relationship with you.

Assignments

There are no assignments for this chapter.

On Deck

In the next chapter, we will discuss the importance of a strong product photo, or photos, in your sales listings. When you have done everything else right, the last thing you need is for a weak visual to ruin your chances of success.

10
TAKE QUALITY PHOTOS

SEVEN SIMPLE RULES
THAT WILL MAKE
OR BREAK YOUR LISTINGS

Surely you have heard the old adage, "a picture is worth 1,000 words." Well, a picture could easily be worth $1,000 dollars in the used resale market! How, you ask? Photographs are the face of your business, after all, and they can make or break a deal.

Preparation
Planning & Measuring
Deal Analysis
Purchasing
Sales

Let's begin by considering an example of what *not* to do. Then we will cover what *to* do.

What Not to Do

Take a look at this listing and its accompanying photo:

Microphone Cables Professional High Quality (San Diego)

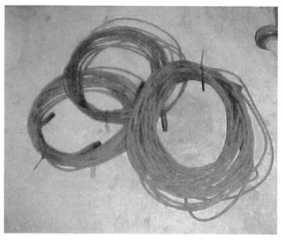

These are professional, high quality 18 Ft. long XLR female / 1/4 male Microphone cables

$10ea. or all three for $25

The listing reads, "Microphone Cables Professional High Quality," but is that the impression you get from the photo? From what I can see in this blurry, distorted photo, there are three microphone cables of varying length, which appear to be quite dusty, on the cement floor of what is probably someone's garage. Frankly, they look like crap and I certainly am not given the impression of "professional" or "high quality." The zip ties don't help much, either.

The person who posted this listing has renewed it for nearly a year now, which goes to show how little interest he or she has generated with such a worthless listing. Every time I see this listing renewed I have a little chuckle! There is no brand or model information, and clearly no effort was put into taking a good photo or making the microphone cables look nice. Not to mention that most people are not going to waste their time driving across town to pick up a few cheap, dusty cables.

On the other hand, I own several microphone cables that are each worth more than $50, and should I ever list one or more of them for sale, you had better believe they will look every bit professional and high quality.

168

What to Do

Now let's look at another example. If I told you the following two guitars were selling for the same price, which one would you be more likely to buy? Keep in mind that they are the same make and model, just different colors.

If you are like most people, you picked the shiny black guitar. It is easier to see the details, such as the pickups, strings, and knobs. Moreover, you can clearly see the good condition of the finish. This can make or break a sale, especially when people are comparing similar items.

This is no secret, either. I am probably preaching to the choir, but why do you think products are photographed so nicely by manufacturers in the first place? Well, they know that people like things that are novel, new, and in good condition. Therefore, they represent their products in the best light possible (quite literally) and show various angles, when applicable, to showcase their features.

Here are the rest of the pictures of that black guitar from my original listing:

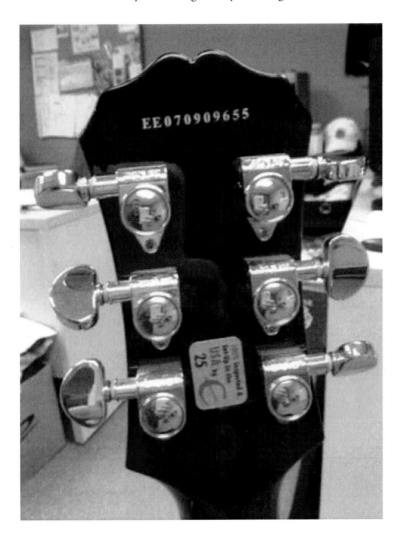

This set of pictures does a great job of showing all the angles of the guitar. It leaves little to the imagination and helps the potential buyer see exactly what he or she will get. Note also that, while these pictures are clear and vibrant, they still fit in with what someone would expect on a medium like Craigslist. This establishes trust, and when I posted these pictures, it made my listing stand out from other, similar guitars, some of which were even priced a little lower than mine. In the end, this guitar sold within a week of the time I posted it.

This is just one example of an important lesson: price is not everything. *Perceived value will generally overcome a price war amongst close substitutes.* This is especially true on Craigslist, where people are commonly afraid of buying "crap" with their hard-earned money.

Let's examine another example of "weak photo versus strong photo" to further explore the concept of relative value. After starting a small business that manufactures sound diffusers for recording studios, my business partner and I needed professional photographs. Before we hired a pro, all we had was the following weak photograph of our prototype.

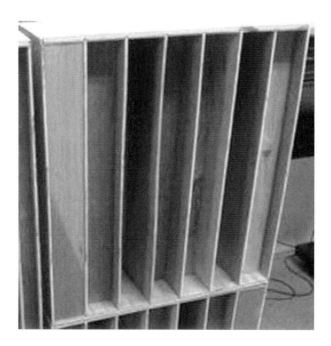

The photo above was never intended to be a product photo for a sales listing, much less for use on a professional web site. However, I show it to you for the sake of comparison. Now take a look at the professional photograph we had taken for the final product.

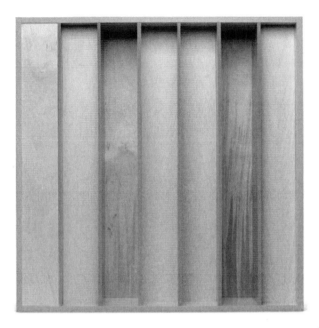

This picture speaks for itself. It is so much easier to see the product, understand its construction, and value its quality in this light.

Here it is from another angle:

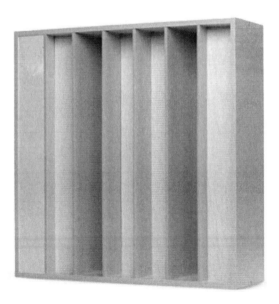

Finally, here is a picture of the unassembled sound diffuser. The reason for this picture is to show buyers what they will get if they purchase the item unassembled (IKEA-style).

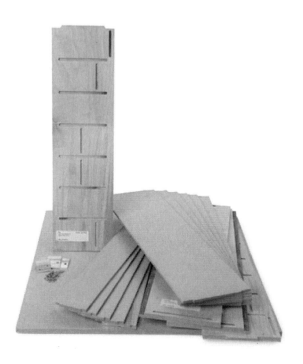

Within the first few months of starting this business, we sold a healthy number of these sound diffusers to recording studio guys, including a gentleman who does professional film and music scoring for the CW television network in Los Angeles, CA. He had just finished working on scoring a new show called "The 100" for the network when he purchased our product for use in future projects. The photos were a big part of what attracted him to the product in the first place.

Can you imagine if we had instead sent this gentleman that crude photo of my original prototype? Even if we described to him how much better the final product would be in the finest words we could possibly conjure up, it would have been hard for him to get that original, lower-quality image out of his head. Deep down, it may have created concerns that would have affected his purchasing decision. How much easier it is to show someone a great photo first and let that take root in their mind and memory instead.

You will find this exact principle of showing the best photo first on car dealership web sites, online marketplaces like Amazon, and even on product packaging itself. Look at any department store or online marketplace and you will find nothing but high-quality imaging.

This is not rocket science.

The funny thing, though, is that I go online and see junk pictures posted *every day* on eBay, Craigslist, and even Amazon (although Amazon has a pretty strict policy regarding photo quality, so it is hard to get away with a bad picture for long). Some pictures are so bad that you can barely tell what was photographed. This is not acceptable, and it generally causes a potential buyer to be wary of pursuing the transaction.

This is why I felt the need to include this chapter and spell out in clear detail what you need to do. Note: you do not need to obtain professional photography unless you are running a full-blown business, but you still need to put some effort into your listing photos.

Seven Hard and Fast Rules

1. Always put your best photo first.
2. Take high-quality product photos (camera phones work fine for this purpose*).
3. Take photos in good lighting conditions or outdoors during the daytime.
4. Provide multiple shots showcasing the various angles/features of your product.
5. Photograph any serial numbers or important markings on the product.
6. Take photos of any damage, dents, dings, etc. to be forthright and honest.

7. Experiment with different lighting, backdrops, and camera angles until you get the "perfect" shot.

*Make sure to wipe any grease off the actual camera lens prior to taking a photo when using your camera phone. Since you are constantly touching your phone, it is common to get fingerprints and other grime on the lens, and even a thin film can blur your picture or cause it to be out of focus. Take the two seconds required to wipe it off with your shirt and you will be just fine.

Speaking of camera angles, if your product has a clear "front," it almost always does your product justice to get a photo of that side from an angle. For example, if you look at the first picture I included of the black guitar, I held the camera relatively close to the edge of the guitar and shot it at an angle. This gives it dimension, depth, and a certain amount of sex appeal. Yes, sex appeal – we all know sex sells. Here is another example of a guitar amplifier that I sold just days after I purchased it. Notice how the angle of this picture gives the amp some intrigue.

Taking photos of products straight-on is boring and routine. You want people to be excited about your product, right? Get those angles going and you will pull more eyes onto the images every time.

A Note on Videos

If you are selling something of particularly high value, I highly recommend taking an HD-quality video and uploading it to YouTube, then linking to it from your listing. For most items under $2,000 or so, videos will not be necessary, but if you are flipping items worth several thousand dollars, video content can be extremely helpful.

For the same reasons human beings are drawn to attractive imagery, so too are they drawn to attractive moving imagery (video). For example, if you are selling a vehicle, you could walk around the car with the camera, open some doors, explore various features, turn on the sound system, and even drive down the street. Everything from the appearance to the rumble of the engine in the background will help sell your buyer on the product.

The average Craigslist posting will not require a video, and as you should already know, there is no place to upload one on Craigslist anyway. You would need to upload it to another location, such as YouTube, and then provide a link to it in your product description. To reiterate, the only time I recommend this is when your product is very high value, selling used in the range of $2,000 and up.

Some Final Points on Crafting Great Listings

Since we're on the topic of crafting great sales listings, let me point out two more helpful concepts to ensure your listings are shown in the best possible light:

1. Avoid prices ending in zeros
2. Keep it short, but offer value points

Avoid prices ending in zeros

Here is a very useful little secret: when pricing things (whether in a sales listing, in a trade offer, or in other negotiations by email or phone), avoid advertising your products at nice round numbers ending in zeros.

For instance, let's say I have an item that might sell for about $500. Rather than price it for sale at $500 exactly, I might choose either $490 or $510. Nice, round numbers like $500 tend to seem artificial and fake, and may hurt your credibility. After all, how often is an item really worth *exactly* that much, with perfect zeros at the end?

To avoid inspiring skepticism or distrust in your buyers, use prices that appear more carefully chosen, such as $315, $390, and $640. Numbers like this, which appear to be more deliberately calculated, are easier to trust at first glance. They appear to be more precise and "realistic," regardless of whether or not this is actually the case.

To provide a classic example of this, you may have noticed that Walmart displays prices like $13.46 and $7.28, instead of $13.99 and $7.49, in their stores. Aside from showcasing prices that appear more credible, this strategy is a means of showing customers – at least in theory – that the store has done everything in their power to shave off every last penny, rather than rounding up to the nearest $___.99. Surveys show that customers believe this, too, despite the fact that we know plenty of profit margin still lurks beneath the surface.

Note that on Craigslist, getting into the dollars and pennies is unnecessary. Just be sure to avoid the "round" numbers like $200 or $300. Do not bother with ninety-nines, either (like $199, or $199.99) – if anything, this is likely to seem out of place and a little too "retail" for something used. As a general rule of thumb, the culture on Craigslist is one where the lowest divisor of payment is $5, and perhaps more frequently $10.

To take things a step further, let me also point out that it is better to list your prices without decimals. In other words, you should use $315, $390, and $640 instead of $315.00, $390.00, and $640.00.

Expensive restaurants rely on this strategy to make pricy meals seem less costly, as longer prices (including decimals) appear more expensive to the average consumer. Why? A longer price takes longer to physically read, and we tend to subconsciously associate more numbers with higher amounts, even if consciously we know better. In the case of restaurants, they will even decrease the font size to make the price seem less significant still.

If you want to get even more crazy with it, you can drop the "$" sign from your price altogether, so your prices read 315, 390, and 640. The dollar sign can cause a buyer to more quickly associate a purchase with his/her wallet, including the corresponding "pain" that may come with spending that money. By leaving the dollar sign off, we can avoid these subconscious triggers altogether.

Along similar lines, I usually put my price at the end of a sales listing, rather than at the beginning, to decrease its apparent significance and keep the potential buyer's focus on the item itself, rather than its cost.

Interestingly enough, all of this works in reverse, too. When you're a buyer making an offering on a listing, or during a trade, listing the price first and putting all the adornments back on can make it appear bigger than it actually is. Sometimes I even put my price in bold when I really want to come on strong.

Keep it short, but offer value points

Keeping a listing short – somewhere between one and three paragraphs – is the ideal length I have found in my listings. Listings that are even shorter can be okay when the picture is relied upon as the primary means of generating interest, but it is often helpful to include some detail about your product, including the main features that provide value to the buyer.

It's important, though, to not get *too* salesy with it because, here again, the culture on Craigslist is one of used merchandise sold by average Joes like you and me. If you come across too much like a dealer or retailer, it can rub people the wrong way.

I've gone back through my own personal listings and printed ten of them (sans photos) for you to contemplate.

1. <u>Marshall Valvestate VS100 Amp + AVT 4x12 Cab Half Stack - $500 (actual sale price: $440)</u>
   Selling my brutal, loud and proud MADE IN ENGLAND Marshall half stack. Pristine cleans, awesome just-barely-broken-up tones, and skin-peeling high drive settings. It's been a while since you could find one of the actual English-made Marshalls, and the tone is absolutely awesome on this setup. I believe it was originally made in 2000. The AVT 4x12 cab is very highly reviewed as well, just take a look around and you'll see what I mean.

   $250 for the head, $275 for the cab, or $500 for the half stack. Head comes with fully functional foot switch and power cable. Cash only.

2. <u>VOX Valvetronix AD50VT 50W 1x12 Combo - $230 (actual sale price: $230)</u>
   Selling my VOX AD50VT 1x12, nearly brand new and in great shape. Sounds epic, lots of great tube modeling features at a great price. These are going on eBay for $260-360 all day every day, so I'm looking to offload mine at a discount. Thanks for your interest!

   $230 cash

3. <u>Randall IsoCab Isolation Cabinet - Iso Cab Guitar Speaker Cab - $300 (actual sale price: $260)</u>
   I'm selling one of the coolest cabinets I've ever had -- the Randall IsoCab. This guy has a Vintage 30 Celestion speaker inside with all kinds of sound treatment and a bass port to ensure proper frequency response for recording and jamming out with tube amps in a quiet space. If you're serious about getting tube tone at home, or recording tube tone at full volume while remaining quiet enough for your apartment, this is your answer.

Inside the Isocab, I've installed a 2nd mic goose neck (which you won't get if you buy this cab new), so you can get two mics on the speaker for recording purposes. This is extremely handy for blending tones and A/B'ing different mics. More on the Isocab below, which gets 4.6 / 5 stars on Musician's Friend!

Randall Isocab -- Essential whenever or wherever you're unable to crank full performance volume and tone. The concept is simple. A speaker is mounted in a completely closed, hinged cabinet with a microphone suspended inside. The cab has 1/4" in and outs, as well as a mic out to the mixing console. For recording, Isolation lets you record your amp full out, reflecting your true tone without waking the neighbors or inspiring visits from the cops. 12" Celestion Vintage 30 speaker. 18"W x 18"H x 31-1/2"D.

4. Bose QC15 Quiet Comfort Acoustic Noise Cancelling Headphones - $190(actual sale price: $180)
My Bose QC15 QuietComfort Acoustic Noise Canceling Headphones are in mint condition and come with the carrying case and an extra cord (each cord not only connects the headphones to your device, but functions are a volume control as well -- they go for $30 each new). Cash or trade OK! $190 OBO

These do a great job at cancelling out background noise and sound, all the while supplying the proven, tested quality of Bose sound. I recently got an extremely expensive pair of audiophile headphones and no longer am using these, but they really are a great set of cans.

The headphones have low hours on them and you could be fooled into thinking they are literally brand new by the look of them, case and all. If you're looking for a high quality pair of noise-reducing headphones, this is your ticket.

5. Hughes & Kettner Tube Factor- $190(actual sale price: $165)
Hughes & Kettner Tube Factor in great condition with new tube! This thing provides some absolutely killer tube tone... check out this shootout video on YouTube to hear it destroy the Kingsley Jouster, the Tube Factor sound brutal at 10:40: http://www.youtube.com/watch?v=uKZNtZ9YUnA

These are $335 new on Musician's Friend and get 4.7 / 5 stars in the reviews. You have to hear this thing to understand why. I was planning on keeping it for my home recording setup but don't need it anymore in light of building out a guitar cab booth, so I can crank my amp now.

This is the ONLY distortion stomp I would ever play with as a serious hard rock / metal guitarist, and the best part about it is that it's versatile. It can just as easily do the barely broken up sound as it can the full-blown in-your-face rectifier-esque stuff, which is great for pinch harmonics.

If you want to get serious about your tone but can't afford a $2k amp and are tired of f'ing around with sh**ty pedals, give this a shot. Cosmetically there's a little to be desired but this unit is 100% fully functional and ready to rock.

6. Seagull S6 Acoustic Guitar - Left Handed, NEW - $360(actual sale price: $295)

I'm selling my left-handed Seagull S6 Acoustic Dreadnought with hard case for $360.00. The guitar by itself runs $440.00 new and the hard case is another hundred on top of that. This guitar was originally purchased by a gentleman who never played it -- there is not a single scratch on this guitar, including the pick guard. It sat in its case until I recently acquired it. While it's a few years old, it was always kept in a climate-controlled home in the case and is as good as new. Most "new" guitars at guitar center have been beaten up more badly than this beautiful, hand-made Canadian gem.

This guitar has 141 reviews on musiciansfriend.com with a 4.9/5.0 star rating. You cannot go wrong with this guitar whether you're looking to record on a budget, start playing guitar, or trying to find an extra guitar for the road with good action. http://www.musiciansfriend.com/guitars/seagull-the-original-s6-acoustic-guitar

All Seagull guitars are hand-made in Canada by expert luthiers and craftsman who are very careful and do an outstanding job. I've recorded with these instruments before and they're *phenomenal. There are plenty of $1000+ Takamines out there that don't hold a candle to these!*

$325 for the guitar, $60 for the hard case, or both for $360.

7. **Bugera 6262 2x12 Combo Guitar Amp - 100W all 6L6 Tubes - $500**(actual sale price: $380)
    Selling my absolutely mint condition Bugera 6262 2x12 Combo Amp. This thing is running at 100 watts with 4x 6L6 tubes with low hours. It's a beast. The lead channel has so much gain that even when it's set at around 3-4 on gain, it has as much gain as my Mesa dual rec set on 6-7. It really adds a lot of harmonic weight and girth to everything you play, but especially single notes. Palm muting the A-string for example suddenly sounds huge, thick and fat instead of like, well.. the A-string normally sounds palm muted -- a little thin and weak, even on nice tube amps.

    This fat saturation is one of the best features of the amp and would suit any metal/hard rock lead or rhythm player well. I've decided it'll be best for me to keep my Mesa due to my dynamic playing style, but don't get me wrong -- it's hard to turn this thing off once you start playing! It's one of those amps that sounds so good you just keep playing way longer than you should (and louder) until your ears are ringing and you're late for your next scheduled thing to do. Would be perfect for the right person, and btw this is a really good 5150 copy.

    Comes with foot pedal/cable. This amp is in mint condition. These are $700 + tax new.

    $500 OBO

8. **REDUCED Les Paul Classic, Upgraded Pickups + Low Action Setup - $350**(actual sale price: $350)
    Selling my beloved Epi Les Paul Classic with beautiful gold top contoured finish, upgraded Seymour Duncan pickups, and recent low-action setup by my guitar tech. Has excellent tone and playability, finish is still in immaculate condition, and the strings are new 10's as of last week.

All knobs, pots, inputs etc. work perfectly. Most folks prefer the classic over the standard, come check it out to see why. Excellent guitar! I've got too many though and this one needs to go.

Price reduced to $350 for the guitar w/hard case. Consider this your Black Friday deal guys! Cash only, no tattoos, no trades.

9. MESA BOOGIE 1980's 4X12 Slant Cab! - $360(actual sale price: $360)

   Mesa Boogie 4x12 Vertical, half open half closed back cab (the highly coveted one), going for $700-800 on eBay. This cab is the real deal guys. Also have a 25w head that I can sell with it if you'd like to inquire about it.

   $360 firm.

10. Seagull S6 Acoustic Guitar w/Hard Case - Brand New, MINT - $360(actual sale price: $340)

    Looking for a killer guitar at a great price? Want a hand-made, hand crafted acoustic instrument with a solid cedar top that will break in and sound better over the course of time?

    Take a look at my brand new Seagull S6 Acoustic Guitar and accompanying hard case (also brand new) for sale. Yes, the guitar has been played a few times, but it is in absolutely pristine condition and might have a total of 10 hours on her. Every surface of this guitar is immaculate, not a single ding, scratch, nick, or scuff anywhere -- nothing. All original documentation included. Beautiful genuine lacquer finish and visible wood grain.

    This guitar has 141 reviews on musiciansfriend.com with a 4.9/5.0 star rating. You cannot go wrong with this guitar whether you're looking to record on a budget, start playing guitar, or trying to find an extra guitar for the road with good action. http://www.musiciansfriend.com/guitars/seagull-the-original-s6-acoustic-guitar

    All Seagull guitars are hand-made in Canada by expert luthiers and craftsman who are very careful and do an oustanding job. I've recorded with these instruments before and they're *phenomenal. There are plenty of $1000+ Takamines out there that don't hold a candle to these.*

This is a $500 package at any guitar shop or online, before tax and shipping, so I'm pricing mine to sell. Currently I have plenty of guitars and have decided that I can afford to part with this one for the time being.

$360 cash for the guitar + case
$325 for the guitar by itself
$60 for the hard case by itself

$500 trade value -- open to trades for other guitar gear, electric guitars, amplifiers, speaker cabinets, pro audio, recording rack gear, etc.

Something you might have noticed in some of these listings is that I included "credibility references" from outside sources, for instance the 4.9/5.0 star rating on the Seagull guitars, and links to those pages and even YouTube videos, where relevant. It can also be helpful to quote "the going rate" that your item is currently selling for on eBay and Craigslist, illustrating why your asking price is fair and a good deal.

Even though these tactics may seem unnecessary, because someone could look up that information on their own, it can be good to point them in the right direction from your listing. It saves them some time and makes it easier for them to verify your claims. Furthermore, some people who are unfamiliar with the particular brand or model of product you're selling may not be educated enough to be interested in your item in the first place, and may just as easily close your listing and move onto the next – unless they happen to see something that catches their eye. This is why I often put in supplementary information: to make sure my potential buyers aren't overlooking some of the value factors out of simple lack of awareness.

Conclusion

Do not underestimate the importance of crafting a quality listing. The most important aspect of any listing, in my humble opinion, is the picture. Great pictures can really sell your product, since we all like nice, shiny, new-looking things. On the other hand, sub-par photography can actually hurt your ability to generate proper interest in your products, and may also reduce the perceived value of them in the eyes of your potential buyers.

Last but not least, remember to craft value-based listings that point out the key features of your products, including credibility references where necessary and links to relevant information. Listing should generally land in the one- to three-paragraph range, and you might consider including additional information about repairs or other improvements you have made. Anything that you can do to make your listing stand out as superior, and which makes your product stand out as uniquely high-quality, will only serve to help you.

As a bonus, go here: http://bit.ly/1o6SxhMand you'll see all the photos I have taken of the many products I have bought and resold.

CHAPTER 10 RECAP

- Take the time to shoot vibrant, captivating photos for your product listings.
- Use your camera phone, but make sure to wipe off the lens first!
- Use angled shots to build intrigue and perspective.
- Use multiple shots to help sell the buyer on all of your product's features.

You do not need a degree in photography to take halfway-decent pictures of your merchandise for Craigslist. However, you do need to go into each photo with the firm intention of making it look good. You cannot accept shakiness, blurriness, or compromised lighting. You must take the steps necessary to make the product look stunning.

Assignments

1. Experiment with taking photos of an object in your house. Take at least ten photos from various angles, under different lighting conditions, in different rooms, outside versus inside, etc. Which ones look the best and why?

2. Rinse and repeat until you feel confident that your listing photos look as good or better than anyone else's in your market of sale.

On Deck

In the next chapter, we will explore another method of streamlining your purchasing and sales process, which more importantly doubles as a method of staying safe. It will give you leverage over the transaction and ensure you have the upper hand with any final negotiations.

11
MAKE THEM DRIVE

EVERY TEAM LIKES HOME GAMES BETTER

Steve's leverage rule:

Arrange for the other person to come to you when closing deals.

There are three reasons you always want the buyer *or* seller to meet you at your place of business when doing deals.

Preparation
Planning & Measuring
Deal Analysis
Purchasing
Sales

1. Safety & Security
2. Efficiency
3. Home-Field Advantage

Let's break these down one by one.

1. Safety & Security

Safety is an incredibly important consideration when setting up a high volume of sales meetings with strangers. When arranging deals with folks on Craigslist, or any other medium of conducting business/trading, you will generally want the other party to come to you. Whether this is somewhere near your house, your business, or some other neutral place (like Starbucks) that you designate, by staying in control of the meeting spot, you stay in control of your safety.

I might add that it is neither recommended, nor best practice, to conduct a meeting at or inside of your actual home, especially if you are a female. Aside from the immediate risk of something happening during the meeting, there is additional risk in having a stranger return later on – whether to attack you physically or to steal from your home, the contents of which they may have had the chance to "scope out" if you invited them inside. I honestly do not worry too much about the "Craigslist Killer" when I do deals, but I still take every precaution, just in case. After all, the unfortunate few who have been brutalized by criminals on Craigslist were not expecting it, or even worried about it, until it was too late.

The fact of the matter is that, if someone is trying to hurt you, it will be much easier for them to take advantage of you on their territory. However, when you bring them somewhere they likely have never been before, they will not know what to expect, and you can almost always ensure it is a public place with lots of other people around.

Choose a location with bright lights and security cameras, or a densely populated public place. This way, if the other person is crazy enough to try something, at least *you* will be familiar with the territory and have more resources at your disposal to deal with the situation.

In addition, you can "beef up" your security detail by asking a friend or family member to join you when meeting with someone. It goes without saying that you should bring someone with you for those times when you have no choice but to drive out to the other party's location.

One tool I always use to prequalify people is to talk with them on the phone. I will rarely meet with someone who I have emailed, but not spoken with on the phone.

192

By getting the other person's phone number and having a brief discussion with them, not only can I facilitate a better business transaction, but I can give my intuition an opportunity to pick up on anything out of the ordinary. It is rare that I speak with someone and get an uneasy feeling, but it does happen occasionally.

Let me tell you how my average phone call goes.

First, I ask the other person a few very pointed and detailed questions about the product (whether they are selling or buying). Someone who is trying to hurt someone else likely has not invested the time into learning the product or industry behind it, so what you are looking for here is for the person to demonstrate a decent knowledge of the product.

If they cannot demonstrate a decent knowledge of the product, keep in mind that they could simply be a beginner and just starting out, or perhaps they are selling something for a friend or deceased relative. Move onto Step 2.

Step 2 is to ask them about their profession and other hobbies. What do they do for a living? Do they like it? What other passions and interests do they have? Most people will respond pretty naturally to these inquisitions when asked, but if they have trouble discussing these things, it could be a sign that you should move on. Here again, though, it is possible that the other person is simply not very social, and might not care to get into all the details of their personal life with you, a stranger who *they* just met through Craigslist.

Note also that these initial questions double as a means of getting to know the other person, which ties into relationship building as we discussed in earlier chapters.

Finally, if all else fails and I am still not sure of the person, but the deal is too good to pass up, I will simply enforce a public location meeting place, where I know I will be comfortable. I may bring a friend with me, too, to have backup in case I need it. Typically, I will suggest a Starbucks, mall parking lot, or front area of a nearby grocery store. These are all locations where ample people will pass by at regular intervals.

At this point, if they have not passed the first two tests and they are unwilling to meet at a public location, it is time to tell them the deal is off. Even if it is a really good deal, nothing could be worse than stepping into a life-threatening situation over a few bucks. Notwithstanding this, you should know I have never felt uncomfortable during the many deals I have done.

Just remember: be smart. I would highly recommend you adhere to the basic safety guidelines listed above as a minimum protocol for keeping yourself safe when meeting with strangers. Beyond that, your strategy should be crafted with a solid understanding of your abilities and the safety of your town.

2. Efficiency

Almost every business has a designated "place of business" where transactions occur. This is done for the sake of efficiency. You should have a "place of business," too, and require that your buyers and sellers meet you there. Let's explore why.

Imagine a busy fitness trainer with several clients to attend to each day. Does it make more sense for the trainer to bring all of his or her clients to the gym and train them there, or to run around town all day, sitting in traffic, to get to each appointment? Of course it makes more sense for the fitness trainer's clients to meet him or her at the gym, where a tighter appointment schedule can be maintained on a more reliable basis.

The drive-around-town thing can be done, but the cost to the trainer (and probably the client) goes way up, due to the time and transportation costs involved, not to mention the inconvenience. For this reason alone, most businesses simply require that their customers come to them, because otherwise it would be too difficult to transact meaningful business.

Now let's bring this back into focus for you.

If you are the occasional Craigslister who only goes on the classifieds once a year to buy something for yourself, then it is perfectly acceptable to drive out of your way if you find a good enough deal. But if you are turning your dealings into a regular business affair with frequent transactions, it is highly impractical to run around town all the time. Lots of time, lots of miles on the vehicle.

Arranging for folks to meet at or near your place is a much more efficient business process. You might need to walk away from some good deals if the other party will not come to you, but you will save in other ways: no running around, burning through your gas, sitting in traffic, exposing yourself to accidents or tickets, and most of all, spending your valuable time.

Yes, I have walked away from good $100+ profit deals simply because I was not willing to drive halfway across town to pick up or drop off something. My time is very valuable to me, and I have firm commitments to my family and career that prevent me from being careless with my free time. Even if I did not have these commitments, I would still take the same view out of principle.

When you are doing deals on a regular basis, you simply cannot afford to run around all the time, meeting folks at their place. Once in a while, sure, but not regularly. Trust me, it just does not work.

Perhaps you have been in the classic situation where you drive way out of your way to meet a buyer, and not only are they running late (or sometimes don't show!), but they are short on the cash amount that was agreed upon. Now you are the one stuck deciding whether or not to accept the lesser amount, because if you leave empty-handed, *you* just spent the time, gas, and miles on your car for nothing.

Similarly, maybe you have been in the situation where you drive out to meet a seller, only to discover that their product is in much worse shape than was advertised. Your three options in this scenario are to leave empty-handed, lower your cash offer, or honor the full price previously agreed upon. No matter what the situation, you lose either time or money in the form of resale value.

Over time, you will notice these unfavorable situations "mysteriously" occur much, much more often when you are the person driving out to meet with others.

Well, to me this is not a mystery. It's why you really need to be careful how much time you spend running around town.

There are only a couple exceptions to the rule.

1. If the other person is really close by (say, less than a three-mile radius) and the deal is really good, then sure –okay –go ahead and make the drive.

2. If the deal is just absolutely insane, like my first accordion was, then feel free to drive a little farther. It might be worth the risk if you stand to come out way ahead on the flip side.

Remember, though: for your average deal, you should absolutely expect the other person to meet you at a convenient place of your choosing. The time and cost savings really add up!

To get mathematical about it, what if I had driven to all of my appointments during the case study I did for this book? Suppose I drove an average of fifteen miles per transaction and up to forty minutes driving time round trip. Over the course of more than fifty individual meetings, this would have amounted to nine hundred miles (three tanks of gas at $65/tank)and forty hours of my time. Ouch!

In the end, from a return-on-time standpoint, this would have entirely negated the gains I received! Sure, I still would have made money, but I would have been exhausted from driving around all the time. Luckily, I did not fall victim to this scenario, and instead required the vast majority of folks to come to me, just like a normal business would. Because of this, I was able to transact more business in a shorter period of time and be more effective in using my limited free time to scout for new deals.

When it comes to Craigslist, I feel many people make the mistake of devaluing their free time, since they would not be making a wage during that time anyway. They justify to themselves that a short drive is really no skin off their backs, so they might as well explore a possible deal if one comes up. Right? Not exactly.

The correct way to look at it is that the time spent driving to a deal could have been invested in prospecting other deals and more quickly advancing your business strategy. This eventually leads to more contacts with more folks, who will eventually be agreeable to meeting you at your location. It also minimizes the inevitable costs of gas and mileage.

In my humble opinion, time is the most valuable resource we have, and we should not be too quick to give it away.

3. Home-Field Advantage

Having the "Home-Field Advantage" gives you negotiation leverage. Whether you are the buyer or seller, whoever invests the time and money driving out to see someone is in a weaker position if there is any negotiating to be done. We briefly touched on this in the last section, and it should be easy to understand why. The person sinking extra time and money into the transaction stands to lose more if the deal does not work out, and may be inclined to settle for less to avoid walking away with nothing.

After all, most people generally do not like to do things they consider wasteful. As another example, most people who go to all-you-can-eat buffets pack their mouths full with as much food as possible to get their "money's worth." This is technically an invalid justification, though, since the buffet purchase is considered a **sunk cost**. A sunk cost describes a scenario where a purchase has already been made and cannot be refunded or changed, and therefore should not be considered in relation to current needs.

In the example of the all-you-can-eat buffet, a given customer's money has already been spent, so it should not be a factor in deciding whether or not to go back for a third or fourth helping. However, most people subscribe to the idea that their "average cost" of food goes down as they eat more, and believe they are thereby receiving a better deal. Thus, they do themselves a disservice by eating more than they really should, and are worse off, for the same money spent, than they would be if they ate less.

The Correct Way to Approach Sunk Costs

The correct way to approach a sunk cost is to accept that the money (or time, or other resource) has already been spent, and therefore the value of that money should *not* be a factor in current decision-making. Bottom line, if you are better off skipping that third or fourth helping at the buffet, then that is the correct decision to make. After all, the money is gone either way.

Let's bring all these analogies back into context.

Suppose you do drive somewhere and it turns out the deal you thought you were going to make is a little sour. At this point, you may be tempted to justify to yourself that you just "drove out and spent all this time and gas," and therefore you should avoid "throwing away that investment of time and money" by working out the deal anyway.

Do not do this.

Whether you are the buyer and the item you seek to purchase is not in good condition, or you are the seller and getting low-balled by the buyer, make sure that you only factor *the transaction itself* into your decision-making – and not the investment of time or money you have made in driving out for the meeting.

Realize that your decision to spend time and money driving somewhere becomes a sunk cost as soon as you arrive at your destination. When you get there, you need to be just as firm in your terms for the deal, and if anything is awry, you need to be willing to walk away, no questions asked. You cannot get caught up in being upset that you just drove somewhere "for nothing" and complete a deal that you otherwise would not complete.

On the other hand, you should be empowered by the knowledge that many people end to reason with themselves this way. It is an unfortunate fallacy in human logic. Therefore, when you arrange for folks to meet you on your terms, any points of contention will tend to go your way when the time comes.

It goes without saying that by no means should you ever take advantage of this, though. Use the home field advantage as a protective tool, not an aggressive tactic. When it comes to asking others to visit you, be respectful of their time investment and do your best to make sure they are not wasting it.

There is a fine line between maintaining home field advantage for the sake of practicality and doing so with the intent to pressure the other person into a different deal after they arrive. To risk sounding corny, this is much like the difference between the "light" and "dark" sides of the Force! Do the right thing, and do not abuse this tool.

Exceptions

Of course, when meeting with folks, if someone is not honest and forthright about the condition of the product they intend to sell you (as a seller), or they do not show up with the cash amount agreed to (as a buyer), then it is certainly within your rights to call the deal off or ask to change the terms.

Remember to always keep your word and follow through on your agreements, and treat others the way you would like to be treated. This means being honest in your sales listings, detailing any flaws or issues with products for sale before the other person arrives, and establishing clear expectations for the condition of the other person's product ahead of time. That way, there are no surprises for anyone and you can have a clear conscience, knowing you did everything in your power to facilitate a mutually beneficial business transaction – before anyone invests their precious time and money.

Understand that you can establish firm ground rules for your business (such as requiring people to transact business at your location) while simultaneously upholding proper values. By maintaining good character and ethics, you will create a positive reputation for yourself and build up a bank of good karma in the process. This will come back to you in many ways and different forms over time.

CHAPTER 11 RECAP

- Always arrange for the other party to meet you at your location, or one of your choosing.
- Maximize your SAFETY by meeting at your location
- Improve EFFICIENCY and reduce waste by meeting at your location.
- Gain LEVERAGE and avoid scams by meeting at your location.

Remember, you want people to come to you for deal execution as often as possible. It is acceptable to drive somewhere if the other party's location is in close proximity to you, or if the deal holds big upside potential, but generally speaking, you should make it a rule for people to meet you on your terms. This is how most normal businesses operate, and it is truly in the best interest of safety, efficiency, and leverage.

Assignments

There are no assignments for this chapter.

On Deck

In the following chapter, we will discuss one of the key elements of closing business deals: negotiations. What I intend to give you is my own practical take on this sometimes confusing subject. Rather than memorizing stale tactics, we will look at a fresh and professional approach to attaining win-win outcomes in your negotiations.

12
NEGOTIATE VALUE

SIX STEPS TO CLOSING THE DEAL

Some deals are really simple. As a buyer, you make an offer and the seller accepts it outright. As a seller, you get a reasonably good offer and accept it outright. Easy.

> Preparation
> Planning & Measuring
> Deal Analysis
> **Purchasing**
> **Sales**

These situations require little to no negotiation. All you need here is to coordinate a meeting time, meet, and the deal is done. Nice.

Can you believe around half of my Craigslist transactions go this way? This might seem unusual, but remember, I do a fair amount of research before contacting sellers or uploading my listings.

As a buyer, I typically know how much I can expect to buy something for before I buy it, and as a seller, I generally know how much I can expect to sell it for. This makes the deal execution phase much easier.

What If Negotiation *Is* Required?

Many transactions do require some amount of discussion and negotiation before the deal is made. This is especially true in trades. Therefore, it is helpful to know some basic guidelines to communicate effectively and maximize your chances of reaching a mutually beneficial deal.

Moreover, in both the professional business world and the personal-life world, you can expect to negotiate with people all the time, so it really pays to get a handle on this part of your life. Successful negotiation takes a little work, but it is easy once you get the hang of it.

Where to begin?

First, to be truly influential, it is of utmost importance to communicate and provide real, meaningful **value** to the other party in a negotiation (or conversation, interaction, etc.).

This holds true whether you are engaged in discussion with a client, vendor, third party, business partner, or some other person or entity. We must do our best to communicate value to them on *their* terms, based on what is important to *them*.

This is an interesting conclusion to arrive at for most people, though, since the average person sees a negotiation as a battle of sorts, to be won or lost, in which they are fighting for position. They have their entire focus on what's in it for them, as opposed to what's in it for the other person.

If this sounds like you, do not be embarrassed. Like I mentioned, for most people, this is par for the course, and I admittedly used to be this way too, until I got into sales.

What I eventually realized is that the underlying logic of value provision is simple enough to understand, which inspired me to change my views and apply this new method of thinking to my communications and business engagements. After all, considering how much I knew *I* cared about what was in it for *me* most of the time, it made a lot of sense that it would be very powerful if I could start communicating with other people in terms of the value *they* could extract from the deal.

When I did indeed begin communicating with people in this fashion, shaping my communications and thought patterns around win-win goals that met their needs and provided value to them, the path to success became much clearer. In fact, my thought processes started changing altogether, as I began seeking to acquire new inventory that would likely satisfy a future buyer's value standards, as opposed to my own.

Prior to this, I just assumed most people would value things the same way I did. After all, why would anyone think any differently than me, right? If I like red guitars with humbuckers, surely everyone else does...right? Sadly, no.

But this is my point: most of us never take the time to consider the fact that what *we* value has the potential to be vastly different from what a current or future customer values. At the end of the day, as much as we might think our perceptions of value are "correct" for whatever reasons we may have, we will be more effective in sales if we can identify what our buyers value and present things to them based on those preferences.

Therefore, try to get out of your own head as much as possible. Instead, get into the head of your buyer and start figuring out what they like. This concept of "putting yourself in someone else's shoes" is not just limited to business; it pays dividends in personal life, too.

VALUES

Over the years, I have developed a basic system for communication that works well for me in the business world and in my personal life. This simple system is based on lessons I have learned from life experience, helpful advice from highly effective communicators and mentors, and key tips from some of the books I have read.

Whether it is applied towards a heated negotiation or a more casual conversation, it leverages proven communication principles to ask for what you want while establishing trust and positivity in the interaction.

I use the acronym "VALUES" to describe the six "principles" in this system (also, please note that the principles do not need to be followed in order from V to S; they function independently of one another). This acronym doubles as a highlight on its central focus: communicating *value* to the other party in a given interaction. This does not necessarily mean being "nice," or rolling over on what you want out of a deal; it just means putting things in terms that will grab the attention of the other party.

Realize that in any discussion that involves a desire for someone to do something we'd like them to do, there is a, often big, gap between what we *want* to say and the words that will *actually motivate* them to take action. By staying focused on the other person's values and exhibiting proactive communication, we give ourselves the best possible chance of forming a real connection and ultimately reaching a win-win outcome.

Below, we will look at VALUES specifically in the context of buying and reselling merchandise on the open market.

V - Value must be communicated
A - Ask for the outcome you want
L - Listen to the other person
U - Understand their needs
E - Empathize
S - Say "No" if the deal isn't right

V - Value must be communicated

On Craigslist, often the only "value" to be communicated in a transaction is in the form of price – at least at first. As a buyer, is the price low enough for me to be interested? As a seller, will I get enough from the sale to justify letting this item go?

Despite this relative simplicity, when the actual meeting to close the deal occurs (especially when you are the seller), it is natural to enter into conversation with the other person about the item being sold. Perhaps they ask you some specific questions about it, or you feel the need to strike up a conversation to avoid awkward silence. Whatever the case, you should be prepared to communicate effectively in case the buyer is feeling hesitant, states any objections, or grills you on the item's specifications.

Especially in cases where you sense resistance, you will need to walk the buyer through the value points in a convincing, but non-aggressive, manner to recapture their interest. But how do you do this? You can start by asking yourself a few simple questions:

- What are *they* getting out of the deal that will cause them to take action? Can you ask them directly what matters to them?
- Has the other party communicated their expectations or desires to you already? If so, can you read between the lines to identify what they find valuable?
- Will the other person receive money, or obtain a new product or service?
- Will they enhance their image, or perhaps improve their ability to achieve a goal?
- Does your proposal help the other person avoid a conflict they would rather not deal with?
- As a seller, how does your desired outcome provide value to the other person? How does your product (or service) promote their interests?
- In the case of business, does your proposed solution simplify a key business process, save precious time, save money, or improve workflow?

Value can come in the form of quality, speed, endurance, longevity, competitive pricing, liquidity, uniqueness/scarcity (collector's items), efficiency, and more. This is why we must ask ourselves these questions each and every time we approach a new negotiation.

The more specifically you can answer these questions, the better. Note that you will be more empowered to have specific answers to these questions if you operate in a specific niche for a long period of time, during which you will acquire information and experience that enables you to do this quickly. Upon answering these questions, the real key is to *remind* the other person of these value points so they can take their focus off the money they are spending and place it back on the many forms of value they are receiving.

Preparing Ahead of Time

In *The Way of the Seal*, Mark Divine explains how Navy Seals go through mandatory briefing and debriefing processes before and after all of their missions. Even though Navy Seals are elite operators and are more qualified than most folks to "wing it" on a mission, they understand the value of planning and rehearsing better than most. As Mark puts it, "The brief is a very precise way to convey critical information to the team. It is also when the team gets to ask questions about the mission and their role. Without the brief, mission effectiveness would decrease substantially."

The next time you are approaching a negotiation, then, ask yourself these questions *ahead of time*. Put yourself in the other person's shoes and determine where the value lies for them in the transaction. You may not have all the answers at this point in time, but a little planning can pay big dividends when the other person starts asking tough questions, or when they're on the fence about the deal and need a little convincing.

Opening a New Meeting

Let's talk about the very beginning of a meeting. I would advocate opening your discussion with a general icebreaker. This could be something as simple as asking how their day is going, making a comment about the weather, asking the status of a sporting event, or asking a simple question relevant to your discussion.

By the way, in the following examples, take note that I always use the other person's *first name* when addressing them (and then again periodically throughout a conversation). As Dale Carnegie once said, "A person's name is to him or her the sweetest and most important sound in any language." Beyond the fact that ole' Mr. Carnegie tells us so, there is a great body of research supporting this claim.

Addressing a person by their name conveys respect, establishes an immediate connection, and shows your attention is placed on them in that moment (making them feel important, as we all do when genuine, positive attention is given to us). Using a person's name in conversation also conveys a level of sophistication and maturity on your part. Remember, a person's name is deeply tied to their inner sense of self – and their individuality as a human being – which is why names are so important to remember and use often. (Note that if this were not true, we would not feel so slighted when someone forgets our name, or when we are "treated like a number" by an institution.)

- *"Great to meet you, Bill. How's your afternoon going?"*
- *"Thanks for meeting me here, John. Before we get started, I'm curious to know if you have any plans for the Super Bowl this weekend?"*
- *"Hi, Sally! Hey, have you ever eaten at (pick a restaurant nearby)? It's really good and just down the street... coming here reminded me of it."*
- *"Lisa, it's a pleasure to finally meet. When did you get involved with this business/hobby/etc.? I'm curious to learn more about your interest in this field."*

If it seems like the other person is ready and eager to get down to business, I would cut it short after their response to this initial icebreaker. On the other hand, if they appear to be enjoying the casual banter, I might carry it out for a minute or two before diving in.

When you do shift gears and get into business, you must find subtle ways to convey the implicit value of your product or service. You could state the value points outright, but this might be more appropriate after you have asked your prospect some *qualifying questions*.

Specifically, ask what *they* find valuable and what is important to *them*, and only then give them examples of the features that align with their wants and needs. This is how you communicate value correctly.

- *"Alright, Bill, so tell me – why are you in the market for a new guitar, and what's your particular interest in my Gibson Les Paul?"*
- *"Okay, John, let me ask you a targeted question now. Do you play clean bluesy guitar, or are you a metal head, like me?"*
- *"Sally, I know you mentioned this guitar is for your son. What's his current playing ability, is he taking lessons, and what style of music is he expressing interest in?*
- *"Lisa, I'm impressed with your knowledge of guitar electronics. Is that why you're considering buying my Jackson retrofitted with EMG pickups, because the sonic characteristics are more sweet and apparent when playing?"*

This strategy tailors the discussion to the individual, puts the focus on them, and makes them feel cared for because you are figuring out what is important to them and then communicating with them based on those discoveries.

Leave them hanging a bit, too! After they tell you what their buying considerations are, do not give them the whole list of features and selling points all at once. Instead, piece key details out one at a time, and continue the Q&A process until you have exhausted the list. If you manage the information flow correctly, the other person will often wind up becoming the asker of questions, curious and eager to know about the wonderful things that come with your product.

Word of Caution #1: Don't lay it on too thick!

When you are in the midst of a conversation or negotiation with someone, be careful not to "lay it on too thick" with value statements. If you start a discussion by piling on value statements like a used car salesman (you know how it goes – "This car will be GREAT for you, because of this and this and this…"), you will push them away quicker than you can imagine.

The point is that a suffocating amount of reassurance usually has the opposite effect, and you will appearing desperate, which is a quick way to turn people off. Moreover, it is a general principle of negotiations that he/she who is doing the "explaining" is losing. Talking too much falls into the same category, because whether or not you feel like you are "explaining," hitting the other person with lots of words tends to *feel* like an explanation – and this can convey that you are coming from a place of weakness, uncertainty, and doubt. If you were confident about what you were selling (or your position as a buyer), why would you need to ramble on as though you had something to prove?

Solution: Like we discussed in the previous section, ease into value statements by *asking questions to qualify* your buyer. This gets them doing the talking, and is an important contrast to simply dumping value statements on them with no context, which can seem aggressive, pushy, or desperate.

For instance, let's say a buyer expressed some hesitation or doubt about one of my items: *"Steve, I'm just not sure this is the exact tone I'm looking for..."*

It could come across as argumentative if I immediately responded with a statement like this: *"But this is the best tone since sliced bread... doesn't get any better than this. Nope. This is what you want."*

On the other hand, it would be more effective to probe with a question like this: *"John, what type of tone are you looking for? Is there a particular style of music you're after?"*

He might respond: *"Well, I'm really trying to find something more aggressive, and the pickups on this guitar sound a little underpowered... maybe I should look into something with active pickups."*

At this point, I would likely go on to ask a few more questions about the types of active pickups he is interested in, the types of guitar players he is trying to emulate, and/or the sound he is going for in general.

Once I've gathered all this information, I might say, *"I feel you, John. I've always found it very important to have a crushing tone, too. Active pickups may certainly be the way to go in your case. One thing I always liked about this particular guitar, though, is how the lower sensitivity on the existing pickups creates better note clarity and allows me to cut through better in the mix, instead of washing out in the background due to a signal that's too hot. Also, when I'm really feeling the need for more gain, I usually just crank the knob on my amp, which as you know, never gets much past 5 or 6/10 anyway. I guess it really just depends on what's most important to you, then – maintaining authentic tone that you can dial in with your amp, or overloading it as much as possible, starting with the pickups."*

My delivery here would be relaxed and casual. Here, you can see how I was able to tailor my response to the answer he provided to my original question. This is much more relevant and directed than making a vague, general statement that says nothing more than "you're wrong, the tone is awesome." In this case, I might go on to ask this individual some additional questions to refocus on other value points, too.

For example, *"Aside from the pickups, how do you like how the guitar plays and feels overall?"* or *"Seeing as how guitars with active pickups are generally more expensive, what other guitar do you see fitting in your budget that would allow you to improve your tone in the way you're looking for?"*

The first question hints at the idea that if the guitar plays well, the pickups could always be swapped out for something else – the ones the buyer is looking for. The second question reframes the discussion in the bigger picture of budget, implying that in order to get the tone he is looking for, he would need to spend additional money – which might not be in the cards.

Word of Caution #2: Avoid giving personal compliments to the other party until the deal is done.

When you meet your potential buyer, if you start out by showering them with personal compliments or feel-good statements, you will come across as inauthentic. They may suspect you are trying to "grease" the deal by buttering them up.

You know how this goes: someone starts giving you too many compliments right off the bat when they do not even know you, and it is just weird. This behavior makes it obvious that they are trying to sell you something, get something from you, or convince you to do something – and you know that *something* probably only really benefits *them*. Time to run for the hills!

For example, when I was traveling recently with my wife and two of her friends, street vendors often approached us by complimenting us on our looks or assumed financial means. This strategy made it instantly clear to me that these guys were trying to butter us up to spend money with them. They might have even had decent products, but because my first impression was one of needing to put up my guard, they never had the chance.

If you have ever been in a similar situation, I am sure you understand the feeling that comes with this approach. You feel attacked in a small way, and your fight-or-flight mechanism kicks in on some level. This is not ideal, since triggering someone's fight-or-flight mechanism will generally cause them to move away and leave the interaction, as opposed to leaning into it.

Solution: There is no need to give someone a personal compliment to preface a matter of negotiation, especially in more formal business negotiations. Instead, simply avoid this altogether and move right into business. You may feel that you are directly providing "value" to another person by giving them a compliment, or establishing a connection, but this is nothing more than a distraction that could be misinterpreted.

To clarify, you do not want the other person to think that you are "buttering them up." We *all* know that most deals we need "buttering up" for are not such good deals to begin with. Moreover, you cannot afford to come across as desperate or as though you are not confident in what you bring to the table.

Inject Your Expertise

I cannot tell you how many times I have been in the middle of selling a guitar and had a buyer on the fence ask me, *"Steve, knowing what you now know about me, in all honesty, should I buy this guitar? You have been playing and teaching for fifteen years, and I'm just a beginner. I'm at your mercy... give me the low-down."*

After asking them what type of music they play, what skill level they are at, and what their goals are for both tone and playability, I can better explain the pros and cons of a particular instrument and make a recommendation. Sometimes my recommendation *is* to buy my guitar, but sometimes it is not. In this latter case, I often have another guitar in my inventory that would be a better fit for them, which I can recommend. But if I do not have a good solution for my buyer, I will generally say so. Honesty goes a long way.

Here are some snippets of things I have said during my own encounters for you to ponder:

- *"This honestly isn't the* best *guitar for your needs. For your style of music, you really need a guitar with well-calibrated low action, a killer bridge, active pickups, and a fast neck. However, if your budget is $275, this is about as good as it's going to get until you can afford to shell out $2,000 or more."*

- *"You just told me that you're learning to play Eric Clapton. A great guitar for his style is the Fender Stratocaster, and I don't have any of them for sale. At a minimum, you should get something with single-coil pickups, which is what he tends to use. This will give you the best chance at emulating his tone and sound."*

- *"If you're just learning guitar, I wouldn't recommend starting out with an electric guitar. You should consider starting with an acoustic guitar to learn the fundamentals and build up dexterity and strength. I don't have any acoustics for sale at the moment, so you'll need to browse elsewhere, but believe me, it's worth the hassle. Plus, you'll be glad later when you move over to the electric guitar."*

- *"The clean tones are a little lacking in this particular amp because of the way it is wired by the manufacturer. If you play really distorted tones most of the time, it might work, but if you really need solid cleans, this isn't for you."*

The funny thing about these particular cases is that the buyer ended up purchasing the item from me every time, despite my recommendation to the contrary. I do not want to go as far as to say reverse psychology is at work here, but let's consider that last example again:

"The clean tones are a little lacking in this particular amp because of the way it is wired by the manufacturer. If you play really distorted most of the time, it might work, but if you really need solid cleans, this isn't for you."

I know if *I* were the buyer and this is what the seller told me, I would probably be thinking to myself, "Hmm... I suppose the cleans *could* be better, but they sound good enough for me, and the distorted tones absolutely rock. Do I *really* need the best cleans anyways?" At a minimum, I would at least appreciate the seller's honesty and desire to be forthright about the pros *and* the cons, and feel more comfortable in the transaction with this seller.

On the other hand, what if the seller tried to tell me that the cleans sounded better than they really did or draw attention away from the fact that this is a legitimate weakness?

"Dude, some people say the cleans aren't that good on this amp... but TRUST me, you're going to sound awesome, especially cause you're such a killer guitarist. You're gonna ROCK these cleans, bro!"

Uh oh. Why is he so worried about making me think the cleans are good? Are they *not* good? Is there something wrong or damaged with the amp?

Now I am on the defensive and questioning the tone and quality of the cleans, both internally and possibly externally as well. The fight-or-flight response has kicked in, and I am now wondering if I should be concerned about the transaction as a whole.

I think you can see my point. In each case, we have the same people dealing with the same equipment, but depending on how the communication is delivered, a different emotional environment and mindset will result. And different emotions and mindsets lead to different purchasing decisions; namely, one where the buyer *does* buy and one where the buyer does *not* buy.

In one situation, it seems like the seller is just out for himself, trying to cover up flaws and make the sale quickly to get the money. Yikes. But in the other situation, it is clear that the seller is attempting to genuinely communicate value, put him or herself in the shoes of the buyer, and do the good, honest, and right thing. This builds trust and removes the defensive guard the average buyer has going into a big purchase.

Understand that you need to be someone's honest partner and provide them with the information they need to come to their own conclusion. Focus on the value that *does* exist and let them fill in the rest. Otherwise you risk overselling, which can erode trust and compromise a deal. As a best practice, be genuine and forthright when communicating value points, especially when in a position of power and expertise.

A - Ask for the outcome you want

We covered a lot in the letter "V" alone, didn't we! What could possibly be left?!

Well, a whole bunch! In this section, we will explore the price negotiation phase of the deal process, which most often occurs before a meeting is set (during initial phone/email correspondence, when a buyer responds to a seller's listing and makes an offer). However, it is notable that price negotiations may occur well into the meeting stage, if exact numbers have not been settled on or one party tries to haggle for a better deal at the point of sale.

Regardless of which stage this comes up in, always *ask for the outcome you want*. This holds just as true in your initial correspondence with a buyer or seller as it does during a final meeting to close the sale. There should be no hesitation to directly state what it is you want or expect from a deal at any point in time. After all, you did set a Profit Threshold back in Chapter 5, right? Right.

Do not be afraid to ask for what you want. Many of us are afraid to state outright the things we would like to have happen for fear of rejection, fear of people thinking we are nuts, or for some other reason. But it is only by asking for what we want that we can start getting it. You might by surprised by how often you get exactly what you want, just by asking!

Remember, the other person is allowed to set boundaries, too, and if they are not okay with what you are asking, they will let you know. In other words, the worst that will happen is someone will say "no," at which point, you will just move along to the next prospect.

Let's take a look at some examples of the language you might use when "asking for the outcome you want."

During the correspondence stage (as a seller):

- *"Thanks for your interest in the guitar, Rose. Since this one is in such pristine shape, the lowest I can let it go for is $300, and if you are agreeable, I would be happy to setup a time to meet."*
- *"Dave, I really appreciate your offer, and I will consider it if I do not get any others. However, I am fairly confident I will eventually get at least $875 for this particular instrument, and I'd ask that you pay at least $800 if you would like to buy it today or in the near future."*
- *"Richard, think you could increase your offer a little bit to $450? $400 just isn't going to work for me, unfortunately."*

During the meeting, when closing the deal (as a seller):

- *"I'm glad you love the guitar, and I've really enjoyed speaking with you. I have to get going in just a few minutes, though, so let me give you my business card... Did you bring the $300 we previously agreed on?"*
- *"Well hey, thanks for coming by today, Bob, I appreciate your time. Are you ready to take this baby home with you?"*
- *"Sam, it will be hard for me to let this one go, but I'm glad to know it's going to a good home. Did you bring cash, or do you need to run to an ATM?"*

During the correspondence stage (as a buyer):

- *"I'm interested in your guitar, but based on my understanding of used-market-value, the listed price is a little high. Do you think you could work with me if I offered you $340 for this guitar?"*
- *"I have cash on me now and could pay $480 for the amplifier, if you are free to meet up. Please let me know, thanks!"*
- *"Harold, thanks so much for speaking with me about this possibility, but $900 is really the most I could put into this deal. Please feel free to think it over and let me know if this is alright with you."*

During the meeting, when closing the deal (as a buyer):

- *"I really like the guitar and I appreciate your time in showing it to me. I brought the $325 in cash, as agreed, and I'll take it."*
- *"Well hey, I did bring the $450 we agreed to, but the guitar is in poor operating condition compared to how it was advertised. I would still be happy to purchase it from you for $375, to allow me to cover the additional cost of repairs, but otherwise I will have to pass."*

Note, I strongly recommend getting the price discussion out of the way via e-mail or telephone well in advance of the in-person meeting. This is to avoid wasting anyone's time. I also recommend only going through one, or possibly two, rounds of negotiations to avoid going back and forth forever. It is often enough to simply make one adjustment to price (if any), and then stick to it to show that you are serious about your valuation.

Sure, one or both parties could always rehash the price negotiation once the one-on-one meeting actually takes place – it happens all the time with Craigslist in particular – but both parties should at least have an initial agreement on price based on perceived value before the meeting.

L - Listen to the other person

In this section and the next two (Understand their needs, and Empathize), we will explore a simple and effective method for communicating proactively. By observing these simple rules in your communications, whether in business or elsewhere, you will find it easier to build meaningful connections with others. This in turn allows you to be more easily heard and understood by the other person, and may increase your influence in a situation like a business negotiation. Let's begin with the first step, which is learning to *actively listen* to the other person.

People find it so difficult to actively, sincerely listen to another person. Yet to actively listen, all we have to do is simply sit down, look a person in the eye, and open up our ears for a minute (and clear our brains of any pending distractions, so we can actually take in what they have to say.

Instead, what most of us do is *passively listen*. When we passively listen, we do not make strong eye contact (or any eye contact at all), and may be thinking of all the things *we* are going to say when the other person is done talking. It is almost like the other person is wasting their time opening their mouth in the first place, since we are too busy rehearsing our forthcoming response to actually hear what they're saying.

When someone else does this to *me*, I feel like they have not heard me. It becomes clear that they are mostly interested in what *they* have to say, and perhaps they have not fully contemplated what I have put forth.

Realizing my communication did not stick or get processed by the other person the way I had hoped, I may try to restate what I said previously in a feeble attempt to get my point across for the second time.

At this point, the other person is even *less* interested and focused on what I have to say, since now they can tell I'm just repeating what I said the first time... and now *they* don't feel like I heard *them*. So guess what they do? Yep, you got it – they restate what *they* just said.

And on and on the merry goes 'round.

It's kind of funny when you think about it, two people intensely trying to communicate their points but not really listening to each other, both getting slightly more irritated each time it comes back around to them, each time coming up with a new way to say what they've already said five times...and neither party ever really *stopping to listen, process, and reflect back what the other person stated*. More on this reflection in the next section.

Simple Steps for Active Listening

To truly actively listen, simply focus your attention on the other person, clear your mind of any pending distractions, look them in the eye (if you are in person), and process what they are saying without concerning yourself about your own opinions just yet. This does not mean that you have to agree; it simply means that you put a small effort into being a good listener.

This practice really pays off when asking the other person questions about *Value* in a transaction, by the way.

Moreover, it demonstrates emotional intelligence, which is one of the keys to successful negotiations. By working this into all of your communications, you will find it easier and easier to reach agreement with others, as they see you understanding and caring for their needs.

U - Understand their needs

Speaking of understanding needs, can you think of a time when someone else really made you feel *understood*? Was it not an amazing feeling? Would it not be great if you could help other people feel the same way?

Reflecting back what someone has just communicated is the most powerful way to show that you listened to and understood what they said.

When you listen to another person's speech, observe their body language and really digest and process what they are communicating. When they are done, there is a good chance you can follow up with a brief acknowledgement of what they just said. This communicates understanding.

Simple? Yes. Too simple? In theory, sure. But in practice, hardly anyone actually does this, so you could say it is actually quite difficult and advanced. This does not mean it cannot be simple for you, though. You just need to practice.

Imagine you just came home from a difficult day at work. Your friend is on the couch and you really need someone to vent to, so you give her a brief description of what happened that day.

Here are two ways your friend might handle her response.

1) Still staring at the TV and lying in the same spot, she slowly nods and eventually says "Uh huh" 10-15 seconds after you finish talking. You are unsure if she really heard what you said or not.

2) Your friend mutes the TV, adjusts her posture in your direction, and looks at your eyes while you speak. Her expression appears concerned while you talk, and when you are finished, she says, "I'm really sorry you had a bad day because of (*reason*)." She proceeds to recap some of the things you said, and you feel heard.

Do you see the difference? Can you *feel* the difference? In the first situation, it is unclear whether or not your friend even heard your rant. In the second situation, there is no question that she listened *and* cares about your current state of mind. It's almost like she... *understands* you! How great does *that* feel?

What It Feels Like for Me

I'll tell you what, when I have the rare pleasure of encountering a good listener who seems to really understand me, listen to me, and care about me, it is one of the most amazing feelings ever. It is as though the other person has truly connected with me in a very real way in the space-time continuum, while everyone else is still on auto-pilot, going about their own business.

Moreover, these rare people are the ones who I am most inclined to work hard for, do favors for, and help out when help is needed. I am sure you would also be much more willing to drop things for a person who listens and makes an effort to connect with you, too.

The funny thing is that all it takes is a quick adjustment of posture and focus, accompanied by a simple reflection of what the other person says. That's it!

To take things to yet another level, you can ask related *questions* that demonstrate you heard what the other person said, further establishing the connection, showing active listening skills, and building the relationship. Engaging in such a discussion may even allow you to determine what the other person's value in the item is, effectively killing two birds with one stone.

Since this is so easy to do, and since it is so powerful and effective, we should strive to incorporate these good active listening practices into our lives as much as possible. I will admit that I am not perfect at this, and I am sure you aren't either, but the more you force yourself to do it, the better your relationships and communications will be. The trust and comfort that results from establishing this type of genuine connection should not be undervalued. In some cases, it can make or break a deal.

E - Empathize

Empathy is what we have been working up to with *Listening* and *Understanding*. Beyond understanding what the other person is saying and reflecting it back, empathy is being able to *share in that person's feelings* as though you were in their position. It is letting the other person know you care about what they are saying, and demonstrating compassion towards them.

Doesn't it feel great when others empathize with you? Empathy builds trust and causes people to want to work together to support each other's interests as team players.

This collaborative outlook is *key* to reaching a better place in all types of business deals and in your personal life. If you build relationships with other people where genuine communication, trust, and a sense of mutual understanding are fostered, you will create allies and an environment enriched by teamwork.

Now that we have laid the groundwork, let's wrap this whole

discussion of empathy into context. The time this plays out in real life is when the other guy is making some kind of offer, and it might go something like this:

Dude: *"Hey man, are you sure you can't cut me a better deal on that amplifier? I'm kind of hard up for cash right now."*

At this point, if I were to call the dude a cheapskate, laugh at him, angrily tell him I priced it at a certain amount for a reason, or tell him to stop wasting my time, he would probably just get frustrated and vow to himself not to complete the deal with me. On the other hand, what if I could leave the guy with a good feeling about working with me?

Me: *"Look, I know price and budget are really important to you. I want to give you the best deal I can justify giving you, which is why I've reduced the price from X to Y. I really appreciate the offer, but I won't be able to do this deal with you for any less than Y. I hope you understand."*

This may not be exactly what he wants to hear, but I am at least reflecting back what he said, communicated that I understand his concerns about price, and showed how I took that into consideration. I am showing my concern for his interests, even while I must maintain certain price requirements. It may be a very brief, seemingly insignificant communication choice, but consciously choosing the empathetic method of communication is just so much more effective than some of the arrogant options I outlined above.

Empathizing takes things a step further by showing that you really care. It's demonstrating that you have mentally and emotionally put yourself in their shoes and understand why they are feeling what they are feeling, for better or worse.

S - Say "No" if the deal isn't right

As the final "letter" in our VALUES acronym, the letter "S" is where the buck stops. Regardless of what stage of a deal you might be in, you must have the ability to strongly say "No" if a deal isn't right for you, or if the other party will not agree to your price terms. This ties back to the concept of asking for the outcome you want and standing strongly behind it. You must be willing to walk away without a second thought if your goals are not met by a given deal.

In the back of your mind, you must always know your limit (how much you will pay, how much you are willing to accept) throughout your entire conversation with the other person. Should the discussion reach a point where the limit is being approached or already crossed, your reaction is simple: "No."

It is not emotional, nor is it personal. It *is* a confident act, though. You need to buy at certain prices and sell at certain prices, and that's that. When a deal you are working on does not fall within those boundaries, well... there is no deal.

With that being said, I will say "No" a few different ways, depending on who I am dealing with and what the context is.

Indirect
"I appreciate your time, but unfortunately I can't work with you at that price."

More direct
"Sorry, I can't accept $260 for the guitar. I do appreciate the offer, but I'm looking for $300 or more."

Very direct
"No, I'm firm at $300."

As soon as you feel that you are outside of your limits, it is much more powerful to simply say "No" and walk away immediately.

In fact, sometimes I'll tell a person "No" and they'll email me a week or two later asking if my original offer is still on the table. This has happened quite a few times, in fact. When you let the other person know exactly where you stand, they will often come back when the time is right.

The point is that you should not be afraid to confidently tell someone "No" when a deal is not right for you, your business, your family, or whatever the situation may be. This keeps you disciplined and on track with the budgetary and financial goals you have previously set.

***

To recap the **VALUES** negotiation system in a simple way:

Create and communicate VALUE.
ASK for the desired outcome.
LISTEN.
UNDERSTAND.
EMPATHIZE.
SAY "no" if you must.

Remember, successful negotiation stems from taking a proper interest in the other person and their views. On top of this, you must clearly show value, ask for what you need, and calmly say "No" if a meeting of the minds can't be reached.

Start practicing this strategy now and watch how your interactions (and deals) improve over time. Eventually, the light bulb will start shining brightly, as you discover you are making genuine friends and closing more deals than ever before.

CHAPTER 12 RECAP

- Create and communicate Value to the other party.
- Ask for the outcome you want.
- Listen, Understand, and Empathize.
- Say "No" if the deal still is not right for you.

Remember, the most important part of negotiation is conveying value to the other person on their terms. Beyond that, it pays to be emotionally intelligent, which you can do simply by listening, understanding, and empathizing with people.

Assignments

1. Find a friend or family member with whom you can practice active listening. Ideally, you want to find someone with something meaningful (to them) to talk about or share. Even better if it is something that you do not entirely understand. This will force you to pay extra attention to take in what they are saying, make sense of it, and reflect it back to them.

   The listening process need not take more than five to ten minutes to complete. Note that you can and should periodically stop the other person (while they are talking) to ask clarifying questions and explore certain thoughts in more detail, especially ones you do not fully understand.

   Once you have finished your conversation, ask them for feedback regarding your listening abilities. Did you make them feel heard and understood? Were you easy to talk to, and did your body language and/or tone of voice cause them to want to elaborate further? What areas of improvement do they suggest you focus on, if any?

This exercise may feel a bit contrived, but with a close and trusted friend or family member, it can still be a valuable learning tool.

On Deck

In the following chapter, we will discuss how to leverage trades for maximum profit. Trades are unique opportunities that often include some amount of cash and multiple items, and can get really interesting, depending on the stakes.

13
LEVERAGE TRADES

THE HIDDEN KEY TO BIGGER PROFIT MARGINS

This chapter will give you the confidence to approach trade situations with ease. The fact is, trade opportunities are great ways to maximize value received from a transaction. Knowing how to leverage this value is the key to success.

Preparation

Planning & Measuring

Deal Analysis

Purchasing

Sales

Trades introduce more variables into the equation, because they often include cash plus one or more items. In such cases, you must determine the relative value of all items on the table before proceeding, and then leverage this information to your advantage.

For instance, once the relative values have been determined, you can negotiate for a discount (as a buyer) or higher "trade" price (as a seller) on *each* item. This is the key difference between single item deals and trades with several items. In trades, these individual price movements can add up to a meaningful sum.

Let's explore trade strategies from both the buying and selling sides.

Trading as a Buyer

The best time to leverage trades is when you are the buyer. The idea is to offer current inventory as trade for something you wish to acquire. When you are browsing the listings and see something for which you might normally offer all-cash, consider offering one of your current inventory items for trade instead.

Why?

In a nutshell, it's often easier to convince someone that your item is worth more in trade than in cash. Of course, this goes both ways, but the idea is to work it to your advantage regardless of the side of the trade you are on. As a buyer, you can potentially make a "higher offer" without actually doing so, if you follow me here.

The way this actually plays out requires you to present your item for trade at its highest possible market price (at the very top of the FPR we discussed in Chapter 6). This follows in the logic of "starting high" in negotiations.

This might seem a bit contrived, or perhaps too easy. Yet surprisingly often, the person you make an offer to will simply assume your valuation is valid and calculate any difference in value between their item and your item based on that amount. This is the ideal situation you would like to see happen, as it instantly extends the profitability of your original investment in that item.

But even if the other person disagrees with your valuation, since you have started high (and thus given yourself some breathing room), you may find their version of the valuation is still a winning situation for you, above the target sales price you might have gone after in a cash deal.

For example, perhaps you have an item that you would normally list for sale at $440 and expect to sell for $400. If you communicate to a seller that its trade value is more like $520, and they disagree, stating they feel it is more like $420, that's great – you just captured an additional $20 over what you were expecting to get in a cash deal.

To take things a step further, if any other sellers currently have the same product listed higher than $420, you can send the other party links to those listings, and make an argument for an adjusted trade value of $440 - $450, depending on the specific asking prices on those listings.

By the way, the best sellers to target for this sort of thing are ones that are asking a reasonable price for their item to begin with. Conversely, if they are already at the higher end of the visible price range, the gains you might get by proposing a higher trade value for your item could be negated by the basic negotiation that needs to be done regarding the value of *their* item.

That being said, I *would* recommend targeting sellers with listings for items that are slightly more valuable than your own. Going along with our example above, if you are attempting to trade an item that you would normally expect to resell for $400 cash, try trading for an item that you would normally *buy* for $425, $440, or higher – and which you can expect to resell in accordance with your normal profit threshold.

Let's assume you bought your original item for $300 in this case, and are attempting to trade for an item you would normally buy for $425. If you were to sell your original item for $400 in a cash sale, you would net $100 in profit, and then would need to buy that next item for the full $425 and resell it at $525 to capture the $100 in profit from that second transaction. Total net profit would be $200.

However, by lumping it all together in a trade, you capture the extra $25 that exists between the $400 and $425 price points. The way you might look at it is that your $300 has turned into $425, for a net profit of $125, and then the forthcoming sale at $525 reaps the next $100. The total net profit here would be $225, then, as opposed to

$200 in the situation with two sales – and importantly – instead of *two* transactions, they are now consolidated into one. Along with the increase in your profit margin, this amounts to serious time savings and logistical streamlining, since it eliminates the intermediate transaction.

How I bought a $4,000 amplifier for $1,025

Here's a story of how the above strategy played out for me in real life, and in a really big way. This is a two-part story, by the way. There is a smaller transaction first, and the big one second. Both were great deals, and together they exemplify the principle of capturing the "money in the middle" of a smart trade.

Transaction #1

It all started with browsing the listings, just like any other day. Scanning for deals, running through my mental analyses of what might be hot to pick up, and so on. Although, I was actually scanning the Los Angeles musical instrument listings for a change, as opposed to my normal San Diego listings – occasionally I will scan those (and the Orange County listings – OC is smack in the middle between SD and LA) to open my eyes to a wider market, despite the logistical roadblocks that often stand in the way of doing deals with folks a couple of hours away.

Such logistical issues are not always roadblocks, though. The very first item I sold on Craigslist was a heavy speaker cabinet that someone drove out from Palm Springs – about three hours away – to buy from me, and they found me by searching the San Diego listings. This is what turned me onto the idea of looking into other markets, because I figured maybe I could convince other folks (whether buyers or sellers) to drive down my way, too, or in some cases, make the drive myself if the deal was ridiculously good enough.

Anyway, on the third or fourth page of search results, I noticed an uncommon listing for a Mesa Dual Rectifier Tremoverb 2x12 Combo Amplifier. Mesa is a highly respected brand name in the industry, and at the time, I was looking to scale down from my Mesa Triple Rectifier to one of their Dual Rec models. Therefore, I had some real interest in this item, not just as a flipper, but as something to use and enjoy on a daily basis up until the point that I did decide to resell it.

It was listed for $1,000, which is a fair price – right around Equilibrium. Very fair, in fact, considering the speakers were upgraded to rare vintage models that are hard to find and have very pleasing sound qualities. But of course, when the inevitable day came for me to resell this item, I needed to be able to profit from it, not just break even. Therefore, I offered the seller $700 cash if he could drive down from Los Angeles and drop the amp off at my recording studio.

This was a little bit of a low-ball offer, considering his asking price, and even more so given the two to three hour drive he would need to make down from LA. In all honesty, I was not expecting to hear anything back.

To my surprise, though, he accepted my offer and asked if he could drive down first thing the next morning. I had made the offer on a Saturday, so his plan was to make the trip first thing Sunday morning. Of course, I agreed and we scheduled to meet at 10:00 a.m. at my recording studio.

The next day, I got there a bit early and he showed up pretty much right on time. After lugging the Tremoverb up the stairs to the second floor, where my studio was located, I snapped a quick shot for my records (not my product photos) and plugged in my guitar to test it out.

One of the best amps I've ever played

The tone (sound) was incredible, like I had never heard before. I fell in love almost immediately, and could not have possibly reached for my wallet any quicker. After verifying everything was in correct operating condition, I paid him the $700 we had agreed upon.

We ended up in a lengthy discussion about music, too, which turned into me inviting him to lunch at a nearby Pho restaurant. Over lunch, I learned that he had traveled to Chicago from Australia to record an album with his band, but they never really "hit the big time" the way they thought they would, and wound up playing small shows in Los Angeles for a while before running out of money and deciding to return home. The only problem was, with no money, it was impossible to return home! That was what had prompted him to start selling off his equipment, and presumably explains why he was so agreeable to accepting my somewhat low offer of $700.

I felt bad that he was going through what he perceived to be a failure (although coming halfway across the world to record an album with a rock band must have been exciting, at the very least), so I picked up the lunch tab and covered his tank of gas for the drive back up to LA. Minutes later, I was back at the studio playing my new amplifier, strongly considering *not* listing it for sale, since it was just that great.

Transaction #2

The same day I bought the Tremoverb, I came across something even more rad in the Orange County listings. It was a Mesa Dual Rectifier Road King 4x12 Half Stack – a true touring guitarist's dream rig, suitable for any top-name musician working on a professional basis. It consisted of two parts, the amplifier head itself (which retails on sale for $2,749) and the 4x12 speaker cabinet (retails for $1049). This particular one was adorned with custom red alligator tolex, as well, something that costs a pretty penny more than the standard black.

The seller was only asking $1,600 – already well on the low end of the price spectrum. It probably would have been prudent for me to simply offer him $1,400 cash and go pick the thing up, even all the way up in Anaheim. Most days, one of these could easily be resold for $1,800 - $2,000, after all.

However, I picked up on something particularly interesting in this seller's sales listing: "cash or trade for a Mesa Tremoverb 2x12 Combo." What were the odds that I had just bought this exact item earlier that day?!

As much as I wanted to keep the Tremoverb, I had to go after the opportunity to score a windfall on this Road King. It seemed fate was calling, and the Road King *is* Mesa's true flagship amp – the best of the best. I remember thinking it would be unreal if I could work out a deal.

The negotiation went on for what seemed like forever. For days after the first point of contact, we went back and forth multiple times per day. My first offer was the Tremoverb + $150, based on a stated trade value of my Tremoverb of $1,500. Of course, I had actually bought it for less than half that amount, but it was not unreasonable to think this particular one, with its rare upgrades, could go for near that price if the right buyer came along. If anyone was the right buyer, I thought, it was probably this guy – he was obviously on the lookout for a Tremoverb, and would probably be all the more interested, given its unique condition.

However, he wasn't interested in giving away his Road King, and knew he already had it more than competitively priced at $1,600. Interestingly enough, he did not argue with my valuation of the Tremoverb, and even indicated agreement on that point. Instead, he used one of my very own strategies against me by explaining that for his item, $1,600 would be alright for an all-cash deal, but in trade, he would need to reap a trade value closer to $2,000. This, he justified, meant that my $1,500 in trade value from the Tremoverb would need to be supplemented with a full $500 to complete the deal.

Had I accepted this offer, I would have scored the Road King for a grand total of $1,200 plus whatever gas it took to drive up to Anaheim, and it would have been an excellent deal. Yet I felt there was room to continue negotiating. I offered a long list of other items I had in inventory as trade to make up the $500 difference, countered with additional cash offers, and even agreed to come up on my overall cash amount in the trade if he could bring the Road King to San Diego.

For all this, the only response I got was a big, fat "no."

Soon I started to feel out where the true "compromise point" was on this trade, though – that inevitable point in the middle of two prices that each party has been holding onto, justifying, and re-justifying in different words throughout the length of their negotiations.

For this guy to truly find the deal valuable to him, I knew he was going to need at least $300-400 in cash. He clearly wasn't interested in trades, and said himself that he would only want to do the trade if he felt he was "making considerable money on the deal." $300, I felt, was probably enough for him to feel he was getting this consideration, so as a last ditch effort, I offered him the Tremoverb plus $300 cash. I would even drive up to Anaheim to pick it up from him.

He wrote back, saying he would do the deal at $375, but not a penny less. Realizing I was pushing my luck already, I accepted and made plans to drive up his direction after work the same evening. After all, I was about to get a $4,000 amplifier for just a little over a grand, which was just plain amazing.

When I got there, we spent a good amount of time discussing the deal and testing out each other's equipment. He was pleased with the Tremoverb, but I had some concerns about the Road King. He had connected the amplifier head to the speaker cabinet improperly, which has the potential to fry the tubes in the back of the amp, and who knows how long it had been that way. To do a full re-tube on the Road King would be in the neighborhood of $300, and if the tubes were on their last leg, this would drive up my effective price by more than I was prepared for at this point.

The grill cloth on the front of the speaker cabinet was also torn in two places, which I reasoned was probably nothing more than a cosmetic issue, but still less than desirable, and potentially a sign of abuse over the years. That said, he *did* tell me about the tears in the grill cloth before I made the drive up.

Still, with my concerns about the tubes needing to be replaced, I nearly called the deal off. We both knew what the cost would be to replace them, and he admitted that they hadn't been changed in years. He pointed out, though, that the amp had not been played very often for the past several years, mostly just sitting in his bedroom closet taking up space. After all, it was far too loud to play at home.

I asked him if he could come down a bit on the cash amount in case the tubes were to blow out sometime soon, and he agreed to knock off $50, bringing my total cash contribution down to $325. Though I still felt a little uneasy, I reminded myself that I was getting an incredible deal regardless and accepted the offer. We shook hands, and he helped me wheel the behemoth Road King out to my truck to load it up.

In the end, then, I had managed to finagle one of the most expensive guitar amplifiers ever made for a grand total of $1,025, roughly a quarter of its retail price, and approximately half of its used price. As for the tubes, they did eventually need replacing, but not because they were on their last leg at the time of purchase.

Lessons Learned

This story illustrates three key points.

First, as we saw with the first transaction, I offered the seller a relatively low cash price for his Tremoverb, but he accepted my offer outright without any negotiation or resistance. This can and will happen, despite it seeming that the odds may be against you, and is the reason why it is so important to send out a high volume of offers to a number of different sellers. The more you send out, the more quickly you will find great purchases for your inventory.

Second, the owner of the Road King *never* questioned my $1,500 valuation of the Tremoverb. You might think it would be impossible to convince someone that an item *just* purchased for $700 is worth more than twice as much. Yet it did not require any convincing at all, in this case. I anchored my valuation high and it stuck.

Third, and most relevant to this chapter, I leveraged a key trade to maximize my profit. As the buyer in this trade, my strategy was to offer an item with an inflated trade value, plus cash (an effective combination). Even though it took a lot of negotiation up front, and even though I broke one of my own rules in driving a ridiculous distance to complete the deal, it was a total windfall and entirely justified.

By the way, the manner in which I accounted for this particular deal on my spreadsheet was to record a $1,000 sale on the Tremoverb, then an adjusted purchase price of $1,325 on the Road King. Doing things this way helps keeps records straight and makes sure items don't "fall off" the accounting report, so to speak. For instance, it might have been easier to not put in a line item for the Tremoverb, and instead just include one line item for the Road King at $1,025 – but then there would have been no record of the Tremoverb ever existing. By recording the trade as two independent transactions, every item was accounted for and easily reviewable. When I eventually sell the Road King for $1,900-2,000, I'll record a $500-600 additional gain, for a total profit in the neighborhood of $800-1,000 on the two deals.

Trading as a Seller

When trading as a seller, your approach will begin with a strategic devaluation of the buyer's item in the trade. Remember, when you are the *buyer* in a trade, you place the trade value of your item at the *top* of the FPR; as a *seller*, you will place the buyer's item at the *bottom* of the FPR.

Is it a little evil to play both sides of the same coin like this? Perhaps. But nobody is forcing anyone to do anything here, and all is fair in love, war, and business.

The next step you will take is to apply the same strategy to your buyer that the owner of the Road King applied to me: inflate the "trade value" of *your* item a bit.

The interesting thing about this inflation is the psychology behind the pricing. Normally, we expect to see sellers agree on final prices that are a little bit lower than their listed asking price on Craigslist – for cash deals, anyway. For trades, not only can you stick more firmly to your asking price, but you can often *increase* it, just like Mr. Road King did to me. His $1,600 asking price became $2,000 in a hurry, a full 25% increase.

But why is this? How can sellers get away with such arbitrary price increases?

The truth is, seemingly arbitrary price increases can and do irritate buyers, especially when the increase pushes the new, inflated price way beyond the original asking price. It just doesn't seem fair – at first.

However, this emotional reaction can usually be managed quite easily. To this degree, there are three points you can always hang your hat on as the seller in a trade, and explain to your buyer.

First, everyone understands that most people prefer liquidity, and in the absence of receiving a liquid form of payment (cash), it stands to reason that the same "discount" is not available for trade. What I mean is, as a seller, you can simply explain that your listed asking price is your discounted cash price and that you didn't expect to receive any trade offers – but now that you have, you need to enforce the increase in price.

Second, and in support of this first point, the argument can easily be made that anytime you accept a traded item (instead of cash) as a form of payment, you then need to go to the trouble of listing it for sale, which is an extra intermediate step – and potentially a big hassle – before eventually converting that item into cash.

Third, if the other person approached you first, you can point out that it is they who must bend – you are indifferent about the trade, and perhaps not even so keen on it; if they are so interested in making the deal work, they will need to play ball. Or, like the owner of the Road King did, you might even explain in no uncertain terms that you simply will not be interested unless you stand to realize a considerable gain from the transaction.

By the way, this third point plays into a bigger psychological principle that states "he/she with the *least* interest has control of the relationship/negotiation/situation." Have you ever noticed how true this is, whether in business or your personal life? The person who cares less about the outcome tends to be in control, and will more easily dictate how things progress. This is because they have less attachment to what will be *lost* in the event an agreement is not reached. Conversely, it is the person who cares most that is most likely to break down in the final hour and make concessions in order to "make it work," even if the outcome is not fair to them.

I do not recommend manipulating others with this knowledge, but what I do recommend is legitimately getting to a place in your own head and heart where you truly do not care about the outcome of any particular deal or sale. This will empower you to more confidently tackle negotiations and master your emotions in a way that sets you up for long-term success.

Of course, all of the above three points sound very powerful and convincing, but any given buyer can still turn you down. At the very least, though, talking through some of these points can establish your initial "boundary" in the negotiation at a higher point, and potentially lead to a more beneficial compromise later on during the negotiation.

An Example of the Ideal Trade Situation as a Seller

Let's explore an example of an actual trade that went particularly well for me as a seller. The item for sale was an Epiphone Les Paul

Standard retrofitted with some really nice looking EMG pickups. I had acquired the guitar with a hard case at the fantastic price of $180 (Remember? This is one of the guitars we originally discussed in Chapter 4, and then again in Chapter 6). It had some minor cosmetic issues, but in all honesty, it looked pretty good.

Not two weeks later, I received an email from someone who was interested in the guitar and was offering a trade. Here is the relevant chunk of our email conversation, which I've put in reverse order (most recent email last) for easier reading. I've also placed my emails in **bold**:

On Mar 5, 2014 10:07 AM, Dustin ****
<ea2c7122da1a338faa9f884cbbfccfff@reply.craigslist.org> wrote:

Hi,
would you be interested in partial trade for some pedals?

http://sandiego.craigslist.org/csd/msg/4353910190.html

On Wed, Mar 5, 2014 at 10:19 AM, craigslist 4353910190 <whfcz-4353910190@sale.craigslist.org> wrote:

Possibly, what pedals?

From: Dustin ****
<ea2c7122da1a338faa9f884cbbfccfff@reply.craigslist.org>
To: whfcz-4353910190@sale.craigslist.org
Sent: Wednesday, March 5, 2014 10:26 AM
Subject: Re: Epi Les Paul (Standard) with EMGs + HSC

I have these
pedals http://sandiego.craigslist.org/ssd/msg/4355239219.html the
OCD is sold, I also have a line 6 PODxt live

..

On Wed, Mar 5, 2014 at 11:11 AM, craigslist 4353910190 <whfcz-
4353910190@sale.craigslist.org> wrote:

Dustin,

**I'm not all that interested in boss pedals, to be honest. Might
have been into the OCD but obviously that's sold now.**

**I just sold an RV-3 a few weeks ago for my friend and got $100
cash, so I'd be willing to take the RV-3 + $300 for my guitar if
you'd like to do that. If you throw in the EQ I could give you
another $50 in trade credit (I sold an EQ-7 last year for $50) and
take the RV-3, EQ-7, and $250 cash for the guitar.**

**If this doesn't work for you, I'd be happy to work an all-cash
deal with you, too.**

Steve

From: Dustin ****
<ea2c7122da1a338faa9f884cbbfccfff@reply.craigslist.org>

To: whfcz-4353910190@sale.craigslist.org
Sent: Wednesday, March 5, 2014 11:27 AM
Subject: Re: Epi Les Paul (Standard) with EMGs + HSC

how about RV-3 and EQ-7 plus $200?

On Wed, Mar 5, 2014 at 12:01 PM, craigslist 4353910190 <whfcz-4353910190@sale.craigslist.org> wrote:

Dustin,

I could do $230.00 cash plus the RV-3 and EQ-7 for the guitar with the case. Without the case, I could do $200.00 cash plus the RV-3 and EQ-7. It's a generic hard case.

Steve

From: Dustin ****
<ea2c7122da1a338faa9f884cbbfccfff@reply.craigslist.org>
To: whfcz-4353910190@sale.craigslist.org
Sent: Wednesday, March 5, 2014 12:12 PM
Subject: Re: Epi Les Paul (Standard) with EMGs + HSC

How about $180 with 3 patch cables?

On Wed, Mar 5, 2014 at 12:15 PM, craigslist 4353910190 <whfcz-4353910190@sale.craigslist.org> wrote:

Dustin, I own a recording studio and I have patch cables coming out of my ears -- don't need em. These would be my final offers. I could also do an all-cash deal for you at $360.00 for the guitar and case by itself, or $325.00 for just the guitar.

Steve

From: Dustin ****
<ea2c7122da1a338faa9f884cbbfccfff@reply.craigslist.org>
To: whfcz-4353910190@sale.craigslist.org
Sent: Wednesday, March 5, 2014 12:23 PM
Subject: Re: Epi Les Paul (Standard) with EMGs + HSC

I think I can do the two pedals and $200 but can you send me some more picture of the guitar?

On Wed, Mar 5, 2014 at 12:57 PM, craigslist 4353910190 <whfcz-4353910190@sale.craigslist.org> wrote:

I don't have any other pictures on me at the moment, but I can take some more shots today and send them over. When would you be looking to meet up/

Steve

From: Dustin ****
<ea2c7122da1a338faa9f884cbbfccfff@reply.craigslist.org>
To: whfcz-4353910190@sale.craigslist.org
Sent: Wednesday, March 5, 2014 1:54 PM
Subject: Re: Epi Les Paul (Standard) with EMGs + HSC

i'm anytime between 2:00 to 6:00 everyday, we can meet to up today if you like, where to you like to meet?

After our next email, in which we exchanged phone numbers, we spoke on the phone and settled on $200 plus the pedals (no hard case). When he showed up to complete the deal, though, he decided he wanted the hard case, and I let him have it for an additional $20.

Normally I would have charged at least $50 for a hard case, but as it was, I stood to come out pretty far ahead and felt all right about giving the discount.

I valued the two pedals at $90 and $50 each (my price), so altogether, this deal closed with $220 cash plus $140 in trade coming my way, a total of $360.

This doubled the value of what I originally paid for the guitar ($180) and I went on to sell the pedals for a small profit just a couple weeks later. In total, I generated $400in cash from the original $180 investment into the guitar and case. Being up a total of $220, this represented a 55% profit margin – it doesn't get much better than that!

Here's how I accounted for this trade:

Boss RV-3 Pedal	$90	$120	$30
Boss EQ-7 Equalizer Pedal	$50	$60	$10
Epiphone Les Paul w/EMGs	$180	$360	$180

Another note on accounting for trades: it may seem complicated doing financial accounting with multiple items involved, but the solution is as simple as defining values for all items traded at the point of sale. In this case, obviously I did not actually receive $360 in cash as the spreadsheet data suggests; however, by assigning cash values to the two items traded ($50 and $90, respectively), a total "cash equivalent received" amount was easily calculated.

If you go about accounting for trades this way, the key is remembering to put the traded items on their own new lines, with their equivalent cash values listed as the "price paid" at the point of sale (your cost). This is shown in the spreadsheet snippet above. Ideally, when you eventually resell those items, you will gain further profit that ties back to the original trade.

CHAPTER 13 RECAP

- Leverage trades to accomplish several deals at once.
- Remember that Cash is King due to its liquidity, immediacy, and certainty of value.
- Use trades to help move along stale inventory.
- "Throw something into the deal" to bridge the gap in a particular trade while still maintaining your profit margins.

Most of us tend to look at deals in a very straightforward way – one person pays cash for another person's item. However, you can get creative with trades and combination offers that are mutually beneficial for both parties. Beyond the benefit of profitability, this also doubles as a way to move along stale inventory.

Assignments

1. Find an item you already own that you can trade in the next week or two. Go on Craigslist and find something of similar value that you can trade for, and perhaps leverage a bit to get some extra value out of the deal.

2. If you have not read the Red Paperclip story yet (originally referenced in Chapter 3), please take the time to do this now. This is a very instructive story based entirely around the principle of trading on Craigslist. The whole story is available here: http://oneredpaperclip.blogspot.com/

On Deck

In the following chapter, we will examine the potential value to be gained by moving commodities across different markets, and in particular, eBay. Even though sufficient gains can be made by sticking to Craigslist, there is a time and place to stray from your trusty classifieds.

14

EXPLOIT OTHER MARKETS

HOW I DOUBLED MY CASH ON A RARE, 1930'S ERA TRUMPET

In this chapter, we will explore the reasoning behind moving products between different markets. Sometimes, it pays to list a stale inventory item in another market to open it up to a bigger buying pool, or to avoid having the same products recycled too often within the same market.

Preparation
Planning & Measuring
Deal Analysis
Purchasing
Sales

After Craigslist, eBay is the next most common market to consider, although you will lose 14% of your sales total in final value fees to eBay and PayPal. There are also other markets, like topic-specific web forums and web sites, where listings can be made and your reputation can be established. In the music world, forums and sites like www.gearslutz.com, www.talkbass.com and www.audiogon.com are commonly used as of this writing.

Finding Alternate Markets

If you are in a different product niche, there are three easy ways you can find such alternative markets:

1) **Google**
   This may seem obvious, but this is the quickest and easiest way to find established groups. Due to the nature of Google's ranking algorithms, it is likely you will find what you are looking for in the first page or two of search results. In my case, I might search for "music forum," "guitar forum," "music trading site," or "sell music instruments online." In your case, you might search for "jewelry forums," "HD TV reviews," or "tool and hardware used sale listings."

2) **Call an Industry Rep**
   As great as Google is, artificial intelligence sometimes lives up to its name (artificial!). Until our friends over in Mountain View, CA (at Google) figure out how to replicate consciousness in machines, you might consider getting information from a real, live person qualified to help you. For example, I might call a Guitar Center and ask one of the guys there who plays guitar every day, both inside and outside of work, where people are selling used instruments online. In your niche, you might call (or even walk into) a store in your niche and ask a knowledgeable person for similar advice.

3) **Social Media Groups**
   Similar to asking an industry rep, this method relies on getting advice from a real person. On Facebook alone, there are countless special interest groups for every niche, and most of them are easy enough to search by keyword. You might need to join a group or send a message to a group owner first, but many of them will be happy to help with simple questions. Plus, if you can get your question posted in front of the group, it will often create a discussion in which

members will provide you varying opinions, potentially maximizing the amount of relevant information you receive.

Speaking of social networks, you might already be an established member of certain social networks where you could sell your inventory, or perhaps more appropriately, ask for referrals – this is just as true in person as it is online ("Hey Zach, do you know of anyone looking for a guitar? I picked this one up the other day, and..."). This might be a sports team, club, non-profit group, or professional network. Of course, you will want to gauge the appropriateness of pushing your items for sale in these groups, but if you know people who share an interest in your product category, it might be worth approaching them and asking if they would know anyone who might be interested. I have even seen my friends and family members succeed in selling things through status updates on Facebook!

Accelerating the Velocity of Money

eBay and other markets can be great ways to keep your mini-business running, especially when things are not selling as fast as you would like on Craigslist. Moving goods between markets increases the visibility of your product offerings by reaching different and larger groups of potential buyers.

Therefore, while this book is tailored on a focused case-study of Craigslist dealings, you should know I actually moved quite a few things *between* Craigslist and eBay during the sales period that is the subject of this book.

Specifically, I purchased a guitar, two amplifiers, and a trumpet on Craigslist that I later sold on eBay. I also bought an acoustic sound treatment wall on eBay that I later sold on Craigslist. Altogether, these flips amounted to several hundred dollars' worth of gains even after evil Bay took their 14% from each of my sales (10% final value fee, 4% PayPal transaction fee).

To illustrate this principle in action, let me tell you the story of the super rare, collectible trumpet I picked up on Craigslist and resold on eBay. In my humble opinion, this is one of the most instructive stories of this book, for many reasons.

The Trumpet Story

The seasons were changing. It was the end of summer and fall was clearly setting in. Every year, I can really *feel* the difference in humidity and temperature in the air when the seasons change. I do not know what it is that makes this time of year so special for me, but there is always something magical about it, something motivating.

Due to this "awakening," I was particularly on-point during the months of September and October. Call me crazy if you like, but between mid-September and mid-October, I had some of my best deals: the free organ that became $500, two accordions that netted more than $400 in profit *each*, and the trumpet, which netted $240 in profit. In fact, I did more than $4,600 in sales in those two months alone, for a profit of $2,323! Here is my list of sales from 9/1/13 - 10/19/13:

Allen Organ ADC 220	$0	$500	$500
1932 Conn 40B Vocabell Trumpet	$320	$558	$238
1960's Crucianelli Accordion	$120	$600	$480
Marshall Valvestate 100 SS Head	$100	$200	$100
Marshall AVT 4x12 Slant Cab MIE	$120	$240	$120
Vox AD50VT 50 Watt 1x12 Combo	$120	$230	$110
Universal Accordion	$145	$600	$455
Taylor 110 Acoustic Guitar	$315	$425	$110
H&K Tube Factor Pedal	$100	$165	$65
Randall Isolation Cab	$225	$260	$35
Mesa Triple Rectifier Head	$715	$825	$110

Anyway, back to the trumpet.

Before I came across the listing, I was already having a great couple of months. Hence, I was cash-rich and had money to invest. I was eager to find the next deal after closing so many good ones in recent history.

One morning, I was scanning through the standard music listings when I saw a post that caught my eye. It read, *"Rare CONN 1931 38A Vocabell! (1931 trumpet) Worth over 1800 if"*

(The title of the listing cut off after the word "if.")

The listing asked for $400and claimed that these trumpets may be worth $1,000to $2,000 or more, depending on the condition. I did not entirely trust this valuation, and the trumpet was in poor condition at the time. You could tell it was dirty, had not been well cared for, and needed some work.

Also, I am generally not a fan of selling things that are not in good operating and cosmetic condition, so I knew I would be in for a bit of a hassle getting it restored if I bought it.

At the same time, I could tell there was a beautiful finish hiding under the grime, and this thing was practically an antique. Other listings for similar trumpets on eBay were going for as little as $300 and as much as over $1,000. I thought, *"There might be something to this..."*

Fine... screw it! I had plenty of cash circulating at the time anyway.

I sent an email to the seller, offering him $140 if he dropped the trumpet off at my office. He came back with a counter of $250 and said I would need to pick it up from him. I responded with another email agreeing to pick up from him for my original price of $140, or paying as much as $200 if he could bring it to me.

He got back to me right away and blew off my offer, and as you can see from my response, I was entirely okay with walking away.

Sent: 9/19/2013 1:00 PM
To: hgfwt-4074514861@sale.craigslist.org
Subject: RE: Rare CONN 38A Vocabell! (1931 trumpet) Worth over 1800 if

No worries brother. Best of luck with your car situation! Take care.

Steve

craigslist 4074514861 <hgfwt-4074514861@sale.craigslist.org> wrote:

Then this isn't going to work out Steve im sorry

Official STAR-K

If you look at the date stamp on this last email I sent to Mr. STAR-K, it was 1:00 p.m. when we more or less mutually agreed to go our separate ways on the deal.

Well, just a handful of hours later, guess who sent me an e-mail making one more offer? Yep, you guessed it – Mr. STAR-K!

craigslist 4074514861 <hgfwt-4074514861@sale.craigslist.org> wrote:

Are you willing to do 160$ if you pick it up tommorow? I just got a 20$ so I would have the 180$ that I need, just thought I would drop this by you, if you are interested just let me know. I will have it with me tomorrow all day because a few people on my campus want to see it. So let me know.

Official STAR-K

He was only asking for another $20, but I really did not want to drive way down to Chula Vista, where he was located. It was a half-hour each way! However, my intuition was telling me that he got back to me for a reason and that it would be a good idea to pick it up. Besides, he did not have a car at the time, so it was the only reasonable way to make it work anyway. Thus, I decided to say okay and make it happen.

Then, all of a sudden, I got the following e-mail from our good ol' pal, Mr. STAR-K, going into detail about how crappy this trumpet was! Really?

Sent: Thursday, September 19, 2013 8:33 PM
Subject: RE: Rare CONN 38A Vocabell! (1931 trumpet) Worth over 1800 if

And all of the pictures should show any damage (although the two dents are kind of hard to see) I tried to highlight the plating emphasizing that it wasn't perfect, im throwing in the 1930's mute and the mouthpeice (both in perfect condition) the mouth price should sell for at least 30$ on its own because of its perfect silver plating. The mute I know nothing about, seems to be a generic. Probably came with the case, that like I said in the ad is in bad shape, but it does work. Just not pretty to look at, its obviously from the 30's judging by its wear and it has ducktape, its pretty gruesome to look at but everything else is exactly as described, if you for any reason do not like what you see, at that point I would not force you to buy it. But 160 is what I am willing to accept, and I thank you for finally agreeing to this, I hope you enjoy it.

Official STAR-K

This raised a red flag in my mind... a small flag, maybe, but still red. Or was it just a yellow flag? A sign that I would need to restore this instrument, as I originally expected to do anyway?

My next step was to get in touch with some horn shops in the area to get a ballpark repair and restoration estimate. I spoke with two different shops, who each quoted me in the neighborhood of $100-300, depending on the exact condition of the trumpet once they saw it. I also questioned them on the value of this trumpet, considering this was on the fringe of my niche and expertise.

The idea of sinking as much as $460 into a trumpet that might not be worth more than $500-600 was a big pill to swallow, but still my gut was telling me to go through with it, and I did.

The next day, I picked up the trumpet from Mr. STAR-K in Chula

Vista, paid him the $160, and then sat on the trumpet for a good week before taking it into the horn shop. To take out the dents, clean the thing up, redo a valve, and restore/polish everything, I was quoted $160, so I had them commence the work. Of course, this also meant two trips out to the horn shop on top of the longer trip down to Chula Vista I had already made. Not ideal, but it still felt right.

During the repair and restoration process, I emailed a trumpet collector who has a fairly extensive website about old trumpets. The purpose of my inquiry was to confirm the exact make and model of the trumpet based on its serial number. Maybe the last guy had it right, but I wanted to be sure.

It turned out that my trumpet was not a 1931 38A Vocabell, after all. Instead, it was a 1932 40B Vocabell, and those were actually selling for more on eBay than the 1931s. Great!

Eventually, the horn shop called to say the trumpet was ready, so I went and picked it up one weekend and took a good clean picture of it for my soon-to-be listing (the picture I posted of it above). I listed it for around $1,000 and did not get so much as a single email for several weeks.

Uh oh. Had I made the right choice?

I rationalized to myself that the market probably just was not very big in San Diego for a very specific, rare trumpet. In light of this, I figured eBay might give me a better shot at selling it after getting it in front of a larger audience.

After starting a typical seven-day auction, I noticed a *lot* of people were starting to view and "watch" the listing. As the auction drew closer to its end, bids started coming in, and eventually the auction closed at $648. This left me with about $560 after eBay took its fees.

Cool, I had gained $240.

After factoring in all the extra driving around that I usually do not do, though, my real net gain was probably a lot closer to $200. Certainly nothing to complain about, but still a little bittersweet.

What made it especially bittersweet, though, is what happened next. Right after watching the auction end, I checked my spam folder in my email inbox, and found that I had an email that was several days old (a little after I had listed the trumpet on eBay, but before it had any bids) in response to my Craigslist ad for the trumpet. Oh no...

It was an offer for *$750* cash!

Subject: RARE 1932 Conn 40B Connqueror "Vocabell" Trumpet - $1500 (San Diego)

Hello,

I am available to pickup today and give you $750 cash. Please let me know.

Thank you,

Zach

My heart and stomach sank. This was just the guy's first offer, and I could have easily taken it and netted a full $200 more than I'd just gained on eBay. Not to mention, I might have been able to ask him to split the difference on my asking price and wind up with closer to $825-850.

I sadly packaged up the trumpet, crying internally about the $200 I had left on the table. But the deal had already been done and I had a responsibility to honor my end of the bargain to the eBay purchaser. After all, it was my own fault that I didn't check my spam folder earlier that week – and this proved to be a *big* reminder of how important it is to stay up on communications, including checking those pesky spam folders!

It was also my fault that I had not been more *patient*. After just a few weeks of sitting on my listing without much response, I got antsy and threw it up on eBay. This was perhaps a little bit too soon, all things considered, especially for a relatively rare item that might take a good deal of time before the right buyer had a chance to see my listing.

In hindsight, this could have easily been another one of my $400-500 profit deals had I not listed on eBay so soon. This chapter's subtitle might have started, *"How I TRIPLED my cash..."* instead of *"How I DOUBLED my cash..."* Wouldn't that have been nice!

However, I still got a cool $240 out of it, and I got what I had wanted out of eBay to begin with: a quicker sale due to the larger number of eyes on the product. At the end of the day, this forward progress is what matters. I had no way of knowing I would get that other offer, and in the meantime, I was utilizing the principle of putting my product in another market to facilitate a sale.

Reviewing The Key Points

The Trumpet Story is an interesting combination of events to say the least. Let's briefly review some of the key points:

- I broke the rule of choosing a niche I was knowledgeable in (Chapter 4), because I frankly did not know very much about trumpets at the time.
  - However, I did my due diligence in contacting experts and trumpet shops to validate my suppositions.
- I also broke the rule of not driving all over town (Chapter 11) by driving quite far to pick up the trumpet, then making two more trips to the repair shop.
  - However, from time to time it is okay to break this rule, if you feel there is much to gain from the transaction – which *was* my feeling in this case.
- I took a calculated risk (Chapter 7) and was quick to respond to Mr. STAR-K's listing when it went up (Chapter 8).
- I also said "NO" to the deal and walked away, after which the

seller came back to me with a final offer (Chapter 12).

- I took good photographs of the trumpet after restoring it back to form and function (Chapter 10), and it seemed fairly certain that I stood to gain well over $100 in resale (Chapter 5).
- I crafted a good sales listing on both Craigslist and eBay that got significant attention due to the value conveyed (Chapter 10).
- Finally, by moving the trumpet "across markets" (Chapter 14), I was able to facilitate a quicker sale due to the product's exposure to a larger market of potential buyers.

This story demonstrates that you do not need to be absolutely perfect at this to be successful. Every now and then, you can afford to break a rule or two and still come out on top. It is kind of like staying fit and healthy. Eating a Big Mac and fries every now and then will not kill you, as long as you are exercising regularly and eating healthy most of the time. Your long-term goals will still be met.

Realize "Done is Better than Perfect"

The fact I succeeded with the trumpet deal despite breaking a few rules is very instructive. It shows us that success does not require perfect adherence to the principles, and emphasizes the value of thinking independently and intuitively.

On this note, you do not need to read this book five times, memorize everything in it, and constantly refer back to it to make sure you are doing everything "perfectly." That simply is not required, and will only hold you back from your success.

At this point, it is much better to dive in and start experimenting (transacting business) so you can gain valuable experience, develop your intuition, and hone your situational thinking abilities. Of course, feel free to refer back to this book and other resources throughout your journey – that is very much encouraged. Just be sure you don't let a quest for perfection hold you back from getting started.

Take a cue from Facebook's mantra, *"Done is better than perfect."* In situations where you feel the need to polish your skills more before using them in the real world, know it is more powerful to escape from your head, inject yourself into the real world, and accumulate the experience you need to learn and grow. The all-too-common alternative to this is to succumb to endless theoretical analysis, effectively paralyzing your ability to make a decision or take action.

Realize that once you get out of your head and into the real world, you will quickly accumulate the information needed for an in-depth, conclusive theoretical analysis. Before gathering this real-world data, though, you can only guess or speculate as to what might happen when you take action on something.

Therefore, we should *acquire the data we need* from the outside world as quickly as possible in order to facilitate learning. This means getting out there and making things happen.

Make the commitment to dive into transacting business on Craigslist, give yourself permission to be human in doing so, and accept that mistakes and learning experiences are all part of the process.

Final Notes

Secondary markets can be very useful in your business dealings. They open your listings to a greater pool of buyers, facilitate greater turnaround times in resale, and allow you to capitalize on arbitrage opportunities that result from differences in supply and demand across markets. Leverage them to your advantage and you will reach greater heights than if you stick to Craigslist alone.

CHAPTER 14 RECAP

- Move products between markets to open up your products to a greater pool of potential buyers.
- List a "stale inventory item" in another market to help you move it along quicker.
- Use Craigslist, eBay, web forums, social networks, and other groups you're a part of to buy and resell merchandise.

Remember, there is more than one way to skin a cat and you can often increase inventory turnover by operating in multiple markets. This is especially true when inventory is getting old, or you need to liquidate and cut losses to free up cash for a new investment.

Assignments

1. If you do not already have an eBay account, create one and start using it now.

2. Find at least one web forum or social network related to your product niche to join and be a part of, if you have not done so already. One day, it may be a perfect outlet for you to resell something acquired in a different market, such as Craigslist.

On Deck

In the next chapter, we will wrap up the book by reviewing some of the key points made throughout.

15

CONCLUSIONS

PUTTING IT ALL TOGETHER

Congratulations on making it through to the last chapter in this book. If you are applying the principles discussed in the first fourteen chapters, you are already well on your way to creating a viable side business for yourself!

Preparation

Planning & Measuring

Deal Analysis

Purchasing

Sales

To briefly review everything and put it into focus:

At the beginning of this book, we sought to answer the question, "How can *I* go about generating hundreds, if not thousands, of dollars in my free time?"

In order to answer this question, we set out to *learn the relevant principles* and *apply a proven system*.

The "relevant principles" also forced us to learn about more than just spotting deals.

We discovered how to conquer crucial psychological and emotional challenges, how to evaluate deals in depth from both the buying and selling side, how to strategize by choosing a niche and reinvesting profits, how to negotiate and build relationships with others, and how to measure progress with financial accounting tools and sales metrics.

Of course, there were plenty of other tips and tricks included along the way, along with some useful "rules" that should not be forgotten – like taking good photographs and making the other party come to you when closing a deal.

All together, these principles, tips, tricks, and other operating guidelines constitute the "proven system" needed to be successful. By leveraging this information with proper effort and dedication, the sky is truly the limit on how much money you can earn.

By the way, I might point out that Chapter 6 is the most important chapter in this book. Properly evaluating deals is at the core of being successful; it is the mathematical engine that drives you forward. After this, I would place emphasis on Chapters 7-11 and 13, for their action-oriented content.

However, be careful not to disregard some of the "softer" chapters and related points regarding relationship-building, managing your emotions, and communicating effectively. It may be tempting to skip over these more subjective areas, thinking they are not as relevant or important. But they are, and they can really make a difference in your results and consistency.

Likewise, do not disregard the importance of proper planning and follow-up. Do you remember the following excerpt from Chapter 1?

> *Do you have a few hours each week to devote to a new project,*
> *and if so, when exactly are those times? Can you kick things into*
> *overdrive for those few hours to maximize your success?*

The reason I ask this question is simple enough.

It is one thing to have a desire to succeed, but it is another to get out your schedule and pencil in the required actions to get there. No book, list of blog tips, or other A+ advice can help you without planning, execution, and follow-through.

Now that we're nearing the end of the book, this is where you must take responsibility for yourself. Realize that nobody but *you* can force you to carve out the time and take the actions required to be successful. To use an analogy, I may have taught you how to fish, but you still must cast the line if you expect to catch anything.

Patience is a Virtue

To continue with the fishing analogy, please remember to be *patient* with yourself throughout the process. Buying and selling on Craigslist really is quite similar to fishing, in that there is often a *lot* of down-time in between transactions. Even if you are operating full-bore on your end, prospecting like crazy to find new inventory acquisitions and keeping all your sales listings frequently renewed, you will encounter tons of radio silence, and this is perfectly normal. It should be expected, even.

Do not make the mistake of getting discouraged when you submit ten or fifteen purchase offers and hear nothing back (or only get rejections), or get anxious because a few weeks have gone by and something hasn't sold. Coming from a seasoned sales person, this is simply what it takes: persistence and patience. Sending a high volume of purchase offers is necessary to score the best deals, and being patient on the sales side is necessary to convert them.

During the quiet times, take solace in the fact that you are executing a *proven process*, one that will eventually pay off in the end. Yes, ladies and gentlemen, it really works and there is no magic to it.

Of course, at times it can seem like there *must* be some sort of black magic needed to get things done, or that the process will *never* pay off; even I go to that place in my head from time to time on bad days. As someone with a generally high sense of urgency, frankly it is difficult for me to be patient. I am always glad when I am patient, though, and I have learned it is possible to push myself quite hard while practicing patience at the same time. Staying in a positive, forward-thinking frame of mind is important to mission success.

On the other hand, what does it look like when we are frequently impatient? Well, we tend to beat ourselves up a lot. We are quicker to anger over little things. We tell ourselves that our current level of achievement is not good enough. We may blow things out of proportion in our heads and see things as worse than they really are.

Now admittedly, all of us do need a little constructive criticism from time to time. Being able to face ourselves in all our glory (or lack thereof!) is an important component of maturity and a precursor to growth. Defeat, shame, and embarrassment are truly some of the most powerful motivators known to man. Truly critical self-evaluation is something I believe we should all partake in periodically to "reset" ourselves and ensure we are on track to meeting our bigger goals in life.

But over time, if negative self-talk and emotional responses become habitual and involuntary (as opposed to periodic and voluntary), we can get trapped in a perpetually negative mindset, one in which we never really acknowledge our victories because we are so focused on our shortcomings. This stunts our ability to flourish and grow due to a lowered self-esteem and decreased belief in our abilities. Our capacity to take risks decreases and creativity suffers. It becomes increasingly difficult to take on new challenges with a positive, can-do attitude.

Thus, as important as it is to periodically evaluate ourselves with a critical eye, the actual time spent considering our failures should be limited to extracting lessons learned from those experiences. Then we must confidently move forward without dwelling on them. We must shift back to our habitually positive, can-do attitude without hesitation.

We should also practice positive self-talk often. This means keeping our minds filled with forward-thinking thoughts, feelings, and images of success; this calibrates us to continuously grow and reach new heights. It means providing ample time to reflect on past victories, since this improves our self-esteem and renews our confidence.

Because all of this is easier said than done, we need tools to use during periods of adversity to keep ourselves on track. Remember, when the going gets rough, visualizations and positive affirmations are vital in reprogramming our subconscious minds. Should we find that we have fallen into an involuntary pattern of negativity from a mental or emotional standpoint, we can use these tools to get back into a positive mind frame. If this is something you are interested in learning more about, I would highly recommend reading *The Power of Your Subconscious Mind* and *The Way of the Seal* to learn even more tools for mental sharpness and self-mastery.

For now, though, here are three tools to keep in your back pocket.

1. Positive Affirmations / Visualization
2. Positive Self Talk
3. Deep Breathing

1. Positive Affirmations / Visualization

This is a tool I began using in college after reading *The Power of Your Subconscious Mind*, and to this day, I still use it to define my goals and gear my mind towards them in an effective manner.

First, make a list of ten positive affirmations. They may include statements such as, *"Everything works together for good for me today,"* or *"All of my business ventures are wildly successful and profitable."* Feel free to include personal goals and other things on this list, too, but make sure each affirmation is written as these are: as a declaratory statement that the thing or goal has already been achieved. All of my business ventures *ARE* wildly successful and profitable; not "will be" profitable. You get the idea.

When you finish your list, close your eyes and spend at least five minutes breathing deeply in and out through your nose, or until you feel an intense relaxation come over you. Do your best to let any stray thoughts float to the surface and clear your mind for the exercise at hand. You can imagine yourself sitting at the bottom of a still pond, if you like, where all your thoughts freely and easily bubble to the surface.

Once your mind is clear and you feel sufficiently relaxed, begin reading your affirmations aloud, or quietly to yourself if you are unable to read them aloud in a private location. Take a deep breath before each affirmation, read through it, and visualize it happening in detail in your mind's eye. Continue breathing deeply and slowly throughout the exercise.

Make your visualization as real as possible, closing your eyes and imagining the scenario unfolding in full HD in your head. Spend as much time as you like in this mental space, and be sure to get all five of your senses involved: sight, smell, taste, touch, and hearing. Make sure to *feel* in this space too, taking in the emotions of the moment. Continue to breathe deeply throughout this process.

When you are finished with the first visualization, take a very deep breath, exhale it forcefully and move onto the next affirmation on your list. Read it aloud, go through the visualization, and continue moving through your list in this fashion until you are finished.

The first time I did this exercise, it took nearly two hours to complete. These days, I can get through my list much faster, but sometimes I will still let myself meditate in this fashion for longer time intervals, because it is so effective to spend time doing this.

Each time you go through this exercise, you will feel the momentum of positivity building up, and it will start to seem inevitable that you will reach all your goals. While there is no "magic" to it, per se, this exercise *does* reprogram your thought patterns and shifts your overall focus towards goal achievement. When you program your subconscious for positivity and goal achievement, guess what? It influences the actions you take in your daily life, and you will naturally move closer and closer to your goals with increasing acceleration.

It is easy to develop ineffective subconscious habits without realizing it, but with this tool, we can intentionally remove ineffective habits and replace them with positive, goal-oriented ones. I recommend going through this exercise at least once per week, or more often if time allows, to stay on track and keep your mind calibrated for success.

2. Positive Self-Talk

This one is easy: anytime you catch yourself saying something negative about yourself, quickly say three positive things about yourself.

The reason for this positive repetition is to ensure negative thoughts are not allowed to run free in your mind, wreak havoc on your psyche, or worse: take root as beliefs. Un-countered negativity is an incredibly insidious thing that we must address and fight on a daily basis to maintain optimal mental strength.

Yet the goal here is not to suppress the originally occurring negative thought, push it down, or pretend it is not there. By all means, let it come into your mind without modification, and explore it for a brief moment to evaluate its purpose.

But then make sure to add in three well-thought-out positive statements. They might be related to the original negative thought, or they might not. Regardless, come up with three positive things about yourself and get them in there. You can practice this silently or out loud, depending on where you are located at the time.

As opposed to the last exercise, which is a subconscious programming tool, practicing positive self-talk is a conscious programming tool.

3. Deep Breathing

Deep breathing is a basic, primitive tool that can be used in a pinch – in any situation – to calm the mind and sharpen the senses.

Simply take several deep breaths, in through your nose and out through your nose or mouth, and within a few moments extra oxygen will begin circulating in your bloodstream and give you the boost you need. It's better if you can close your eyes or get to a quiet place where you can do this alone. But even if you cannot, just remember to breathe deep from the diaphragm and your body will do the rest.

This may seem deceptively simple, but like former U.S. Navy Seal Commander Mark Divine points out in his book, *The Way of the Seal,* Navy SEALS (our military's most elite operators) use this exact technique to maintain optimal strength, control, and resilience under fire. You, too, can "maintain calm under fire" when feeling stressed with deep breathing.

Signing Off

The above self-management tools have been very helpful for me in practicing patience, calibrating a positive mindset, and ultimately in reaching both my personal and professional goals.

This is why I have chosen to write about them in this last and final section of the book: I want you to remember them and use them often. They are great for warding off periodic self-doubt and negativity, and will help you generate strong internal momentum in the direction of success.

Thank you for taking the time to read *The Key to Making Money on Craigslist*. I wish you all the best luck, fortune, health, and happiness.

***

Appendix A

Steve's sales data, Jun – Dec 2013

Sold	Item	Buy	Sell	Net
12/30	Auralex Max-Wall 420 Charcoal	$127.50	$220.00	$92.50
12/24	Bugera 6262 2x12 Combo 4-6L6 amp	$280.00	$380.00	$100.00
12/18	135 NOS Tubes from AeroEngineer	$115.00	$82.00	($33.00)
12/17	Lowrey L66 Mardi Gras Genie Organ	$60.00	$260.00	$200.00
12/15	Epi Les Paul Standard w/Hard Case	$235.00	$350.00	$115.00
12/4	dbx 166XL Compressor	$30.00	$30.00	$0.00
12/3	Krank Rev Jr Amp Head	$400.00	$430.00	$30.00
12/1	Taylor Acoustic Guitar	$135.00	$300.00	$165.00
11/30	Furman RP-8 Power Conditioner	$20.00	$40.00	$20.00
11/22	Epiphone Les Paul w/Hard Case	$250.00	$350.00	$100.00
11/21	Road Ready 6-Space Rack Case	$70.00	$100.00	$30.00
11/17	Korg PB Tuner	$50.00	$37.24	($12.76)
11/14	Mesa 4x12 Cab Half Open Half Closed	$300.00	$360.00	$60.00
11/4	Seagull S6 Acoustic w/Hardcase - Lefty	$160.00	$295.00	$135.00
11/2	Furman PL-8 Power Conditioner	$50.00	$50.00	$0.00
10/19	Allen Organ ADC 220	$0.00	$500.00	$500.00
10/17	1932 Conn 40B Vocabell Trumpet	$320.00	$558.00	$238.00
10/12	1960's Crucianelli Accordion	$120.00	$600.00	$480.00

10/11	Marshall Valvestate 100 MIE SS Head	$100.00	$200.00	$100.00
10/11	Marshall AVT 4x12 Slant Cab MIE	$120.00	$240.00	$120.00
9/28	BBE Sonic Maximizer	$30.00	$30.00	$0.00
9/23	Art VLA II Leveling Amplifer	$239.00	$220.00	($19.00)
9/22	Vox AD50VT 50 Watt 1x12 Combo	$120.00	$230.00	$110.00
9/13	Universal Accordion	$145.00	$600.00	$455.00
9/12	Taylor 110 Acoustic Guitar	$315.00	$425.00	$110.00
9/6	Hughes and Kettner Tube Factor Pedal	$100.00	$165.00	$65.00
9/6	Randall IsoCab	$225.00	$260.00	$35.00
9/1	Mesa Triple Rectifier Head	$715.00	$825.60	$110.60
8/29	New Seagull S6 w/Hardcase	$225.00	$340.00	$115.00
8/26	MXL 3000 Mic Package	$129.00	$155.00	$26.00
8/1	Mesa Tremoverb 2x12 Combo Amp	$700.00	$1,000.00	$300.00
7/9	Bose QC15 Headphones	$120.00	$180.00	$60.00
6/24	EL34 Tubes	$84.00	$43.86	($40.14)
6/8	Vox NT50 Tube Amp Head	$400.00	$385.00	($15.00)
6/3	Marshall JCM 900 1960A Slant Cab	$225.00	$300.00	$75.00
	Totals (Gross Margin ~37%):	**$6,714.50**	**$10,541.70**	$3,827.20

APPENDIX B

CALCULATING IMPORTANT FINANCIAL METRICS

Let's do something fun together. We will learn to calculate some financial statistics to help you better understand thresholds, and to gain additional insight into analyzing your business from new perspectives. Specifically, we will cover the following metrics and use my own history as an example to calculate and interpret each of them (note, my sales data for these calculations is listed in Appendix A).

1. Avg. Profit/Transaction (Profit Threshold)
2. Net Profit Margin
3. Return on Time (ROT)
4. Return on Investment (ROI)

1. Avg. Profit/Transaction

How to Calculate: This is closely related to what we covered in Chapter 5: the Profit Threshold. The difference is that Profit Threshold is a goal set for an individual transaction; Avg. Profit/Transactionis a calculation of average profit over the course of several completed transactions. These are both measured as a *dollar amount*. Over time, we can calculate the actual average by simply dividing total profit by the total number of transactions.

Total Profit / Total # Transactions = **Avg. Profit/Transaction**

<u>My Data</u>: To use me as an example: In all deals I made, spanning my first seven months of buying and reselling, I generated $3,827.20 in net profit over the course of thirty-five transactions. This means I was averaging about five transactions per month, or a little more than one a week.

Five transactions represented a small loss, and three of them broke dead even. The remaining twenty-seven were profitable. My *Avg. Profit/Transaction* over the whole bunch works out to $109.35. (It is interesting to observe that my actual Avg. Profit/Transaction here comes very close to my target Profit Threshold of $100 per transaction.)

$3,827.20 / 35 transactions = **$109.35/transaction**

My really big, profitable flips helped keep this number over $100/transaction, whereas the zeros and negatives drew it down. In the middle of the bell curve are the meat of my transactions, and they do tend to hover right around $100 on average.

<u>Importance</u>: As we discussed in Chapter 5, setting a *Profit Threshold* and understanding *Avg. Profit/Transaction* is important from a basic, day-to-day "Is this deal worth it?" standpoint. Over time, you should calculate your average simply to monitor your progress.

2. Net Profit Margin (%)

<u>How to Calculate</u>: This term describes the *percentage* of a sales total, or group of sales totals, that represents the profit earned. It is calculated by dividing total profit by total sales.

Total Profit / Total Sales = **Net Profit Margin**

<u>My Data</u>: For the same six month period described above, my *Net Profit Margin* on sales was 36.31%. This is calculated by dividing my net profit ($3,827.20) by total sales ($10,541.70).

$$\$3,827.20 / \$10,541.70 = 0.36305, \text{ or } \mathbf{36.31\%}$$

I always like having a handle on Net Profit Margin, because it very directly describes the amount of profit gained in relation to the total amount received from a sale. This makes for an easy and simplified way to understand my big picture performance, especially across multiple transactions.

Importance: Whereas Profit Threshold answers the question, "Is this deal worth it?" Net Profit Margin answers the question, "How much do I have to invest in order to *hit* my profit threshold?" One of my friends, for example, frequently hits his profit threshold of $100 but generally deals in more expensive items – items that require an initial investment of $600 or more.

If you purchase an item for $600 and resell it for $700, by all means this is still a good deal and yes, you will be hitting your Profit Threshold. However, your Net Profit Margin will be just 14.29%, and in the long run, a lower profit margin means you are tying up more capital in inventory in order to achieve the gains you are after. To best leverage your operating capital, you should try to maintain a Net Profit Margin of at least 20-25%.

3. *Return on Time (ROT - $)*

How to Calculate: This term describes the *dollar amount* you earn per unit of time invested, normally measured in hours. It is calculated by dividing total profit by the number of hours spent researching, corresponding, and ultimately executing deals.

$$\text{Total Profit} / \#\text{Hrs Invested} = \mathbf{ROT} \text{ ("Hourly Wage")}$$

My Data: Over the entire life cycle of purchasing and reselling an individual item, I invest an average of forty minutes scanning and posting listings, twenty minutes corresponding with potential buyers/sellers, and thirty minutes conducting actual sales meetings, including transportation time.

With approximately an hour and a half invested in each transaction, my ROT for the six-month period in question works out to $72.90/hr across the thirty-five transactions I completed.

$$35 \text{ transactions} * 90 \text{ minutes each} = 3{,}150 \text{ minutes}$$
$$3{,}150 \text{ minutes} / 60 \text{ minutes/hr} = 52.5 \text{ hrs}$$

$$\$3{,}827.20 / 52.5 \text{ hrs} = \mathbf{\$72.90/hr}$$

This is a reasonable "hourly wage" for a side project, and demonstrates the value of being efficient with your time.

Importance: Since time is such a valuable resource, ROT is crucial to measure and understand. It answers the question, "Is reselling on Craigslist the best use of my free time?" If you work full time and are selling on Craigslist in your spare time, like I am, ROT might be even more important than any of the other financial metrics we are exploring.

This is because there is an *Opportunity Cost* to spending your time pursuing sales on Craigslist, which is equal to the value of your next best alternative use of time. Whether this next best alternative is a money-making activity or something for leisure, it is important to consider the value foregone in order to pursue a given activity.

Anytime we find that the value of an alternative way to spend our time is higher than the way we *are* spending our time, we either need to improve our efficiency with the current activity or consider discontinuing it altogether. Personally, should my ROT for Craigslist sales ever drop below $40/hour, I will most likely pursue other activities instead. Similarly, if it ever becomes apparent that I can earn significantly more than $72.90/hour by pursuing an alternative activity in my free time, I would consider re-delegating my time to that new alternative.

That being said, exceptions can be made while you are in the learning curve or start-up phase of a new project. Given the amount of time required to understand and implement something new, your ROT will naturally improve with time, and hence it is more "accurate" to calculate yours once you have been actively selling on Craigslist for a few months, rather than in the beginning.

4. Return on Investment (ROI - %)

How to Calculate: Similar to Net Profit Margin, your ROI tells you how hard your dollars are working for you – but from a purchasing standpoint, as opposed to a sales standpoint. It is a *percentage* calculated by dividing total profit by total dollars invested. In other words, how many dollars are being "added" or "returned" to you for each dollar you invest?

Total Profit / Total Dollars Invested = **ROI**

My Data: My financial ROI for this time period is easy enough to calculate, and will tell us what percentage of dollars came back to me in the form of profit from my total investment of $6,714.50.

$3,827.20 / $6,714.50 = **56.99%**

Importance: ROI is our final method for measuring performance when selling on Craigslist. It is such a standardized financial measure that no discussion of profitability would be complete without it. It answers the question, "Is this the best way to invest my money?"

When we talk about the "return" provided by interest earned on savings accounts, stocks and bonds, and related financial instruments, we are talking about ROI – and normally on an annual basis. Historically speaking, savings accounts have had interest rates that earn anywhere from below 1% to over 5%, whereas long-time players of the stock market might expect a 7% average return each year.

The value of knowing this information is for the sake of comparison. The idea of achieving a 56.99% ROI in a matter of seven months on Craigslist (an annualized rate of ~ 107%) is clearly superior to earning 7% or less each year from these other investments.

(However, the advantage to these other forms of investment is that they are *passive,* meaning they require no attention from the investor, whereas buying and selling on Craigslist does require active effort. Additionally, many of these other investment vehicles offer *higher liquidity* than selling on Craigslist, making it easier to cash out at any time.)

Appendix C

The shrinking profit margin phenomenon

The purpose of this appendix is to illustrate, in more depth, a mathematical concept referred to in Chapter 6. This phenomenon demonstrates how two deals that yield the exact same net profit *total* can have completely different net profit *margins*, and why these margins shrink as the acquisition cost of an item increases. In other words, this is additional support for the argument that you should try to buy as low as possible.

To illustrate this phenomenon, consider two resale scenarios:

Scenario 1: Buy *Lower*, Sell Low
Item A is purchased at $180 and resold for $280.
Net Profit = $100
Profit Margin = $100 / $280 = **35.71%**

Scenario 2: Buy High, Sell *Higher*
Item A is purchased at $400 and resold for $500.
Net Profit = $100
Profit Margin = $100 / $500 = **20.00%**

Notice how in both cases you net $100. Therefore, it is tempting to assume that these scenarios are "equally profitable." However, this isn't really the case.

The difference is that in Scenario 1, you have less money invested, so the profit is more significant because you are realizing a greater return on your investment. In layman's terms, you are getting more money out for every dollar you put in. This is what you should aim for, because it means you are making more with less, and over time, it will allow you to make a greater number of profitable transactions and build up a bigger profit pool.

This concept is even easier to understand when comparing two items with vastly different values:

Scenario 3: Buy *Lower*, Sell Low
Item A is purchased at $100 and resold for $200.
Net Profit = $100
Profit Margin = $100 / $200 = **50.00%**

Scenario 4: Buy High, Sell *Higher*
Item B is purchased at $900 and resold for $1,000.
Net Profit = $100
Profit Margin = $100 / $1,000 = **10.00%**

Here again, our net profit is $100 in both cases. However, the "cost" of that profit varies significantly, since Scenario 3 only required a $100 investment to obtain said profit, whereas Scenario 4 required a whopping $900. You can imagine how much faster your business can be grown by trying to find deals more like Scenario 3.

This is probably obvious, but you could (in theory) create nine Scenario 3's – by purchasing nine items at $100 each, potentially leading to $900 in profit – with the same up-front investment required for Scenario 4, which we see will only yield $100.

By the way, Scenario 1 illustrates my personal average during the first six months of buying and reselling almost exactly. My average cost for a new item was a little under $180, and my average sale price was almost exactly $280. This low cost of acquisition was part of what allowed me to ramp up more quickly, leveraging the power of greater profit margins and making my money grow faster as a result.

Notably, I will still invest well over $180 into new inventory if I stand to gain $100 or more – a hundred bucks is a hundred bucks, after all. But whenever possible, it is preferable to aim for the lower-investment deals at higher margins.

The reason this appendix did not belong in Chapter 6 is because I did not want to confuse the idea of "buying lower for improved profit margins" (illustrated here) with Chapter 6's core principle of "buying lower than equilibrium to facilitate competitively priced sales."

These two concepts share the idea of buying "low" but are really two quite different focuses. In this appendix, the lesson learned is of a strategic nature: it suggests we should focus our overall efforts in buying and selling on certain, lower-priced items within a niche, if at all possible, to maximize growth over time. On the other hand, the concept of buying lower in Chapter 6 is about properly setting the stage for a successful, individual resale; and may be applied to both high and low margin deals, including all scenarios listed in this appendix.

APPENDIX D

THE SHRINKING FUNCTIONAL
PRICE RANGE PHENOMENON

As we discussed in Chapter 6, items that undergo high levels of depreciation tend to have wider functional price ranges (and offer more opportunity for resellers to capitalize on the ends of these ranges). Conversely, we also discussed how items that depreciate less tend to have narrower functional price ranges.

To review the explanation for these differences:

The lower an item sells for on the used market compared to its price new, the greater the degree of subjectivity in setting a sale price (mostly due to confusion or differing opinions about the actual amount of depreciation), and thus the greater the fluctuations that will be in observed in prices on the actual resale market.

When something has already lost half its value, for example, some folks may not realize this and price closer to the original retail price, while others may feel it's already so far down the tubes that they might as well price that item even lower to move it along quickly.

However, something that has only lost a small portion of its original value is unlikely to be priced extremely low unless the seller is truly desperate for fast cash, and is unlikely to be priced much higher either, since moving the price up when it's already so close to its retail price may encourage buyers to simply purchase that item new instead of used.

I have broken this concept down into a rough formula to illustrate how it works, which may help in further analyzing your Equilibrium

Price estimate as compared to the item's original price. The numbers chosen for this formula result from my own experiences working with price ranges over the course of many transactions, and may vary a little bit from niche to niche. There are two steps, and while they look relatively complex when written down as formulas, the math is actually quite simple.

By the way, if you are not a math whiz and the next few pages look intimidating, take comfort in the fact that the material in this appendix is optional. It may help solidify what I am talking about for those of you who do enjoy math, but if not, you can take my word that when items sell closer to their original prices, functional price ranges for those items shrink along with your opportunity to capitalize on deals.

Here is the formula, starting with its variable definitions:

Definitions:
E = Equilibrium Price estimate
T = (Constant) Dollar amount of your profit threshold
P_U = Median Used Price = $[(2E - T) * 0.5]$
P_N = Price New
D = Depreciation Percentage = $[1 - (E / P_N)]$
C = (Constant) Estimated Percentage of Price Fluctuation around P_U
EPRA = Expected Price Range Adjustment (percentage)
FPR = Functional Price Range

E is equal to your best Equilibrium Price estimate, and T is equal to your profit threshold. In my case, this is $100, so we will set T = $100.

P_U is a special variable I have come up with to explain the "midpoint" that should occur between my target sales price (equal to E) and target purchase price (equal to $E - T$). The formula $[(2E - T) * 0.5]$ gives the exact midpoint between these two prices, and represents the central "pivot" point around which our theoretical Functional Price Range operates. This is necessarily different from the Equilibrium Price, because here we are assuming that Equilibrium is nearer the upper boundary of the Functional Price Range.

P_N is the price the item retails for brand new. To clarify, this is not necessarily MSRP, but the actual price at which it is sold on the market by retailers and distributors. You may need to calculate an average for this variable if different retailers sell the same item at different prices; I would typically recommend sticking with the *lower* of the prices amongst retailers, though, to be on the safe side.

D is the percentage of depreciation realized at Equilibrium for an item, on average, compared to its new price P_N. The formula $[1 - (E / P_N)]$ gives us the exact number.

C is a constant that we must define arbitrarily, and represents the percentage of "swing," or price fluctuations, we expect to see relative to the value of depreciation (D) already realized. Of course, as this is a constant, this percentage stays equal for all levels of depreciation; but you will still notice that, regardless of the value chosen, the effects of the shrinking price range will still be present as D decreases – just to a greater or lesser degree.

In my case, I will set $C = 0.25$, reflecting my finding that most functional price ranges deviate about +/- 25% from *the amount of depreciation already realized* (D) for most products on the used market, at least in my niche. Certain types of products or niches may require adjustment of this constant, but this can generally only be learned through experience.

EPRA is the percentage you will both add and subtract from (P_U / P_N) to create your Functional Price Range.

FPR is the functional price range itself, which is an estimate based off the values chosen for the above variables.

Walking through the formulas:

1. Define E, T, C, and P_N
2. $P_U = [(2E - T) * 0.5]$
3. $D = [1 - (E / P_N)]$
4. $EPRA = D * C$
5. $FPR = [(P_U / P_N) +/-EPRA] * P_N$

Here is how the formulas look for Epiphone Les Paul Standard guitars that come with a hard case:

Epiphone Les Paul Standard
Note that the base retail price of this guitar is approximately $500, and a new hard case to go with it is $80.

1. $E = \$350$, $T = \$100$, $C = 0.25$, $P_N = \$580$
2. $P_U = [(2*\$350 - \$100) * 0.5] = \$300$
3. $D = [1 - (\$350 / \$580)] = 0.3965$
4. $EPRA = (0.3965) * (0.25) = 0.0991$, or **9.91%**
5. $FPR = [(P_U / P_N) +/-EPRA] * P_N =$

> Part A: $[(P_U / P_N) +EPRA] * P_N =$
> $[(\$300 / \$580) + 0.0991] * \$580 = $ **$357.48**

> Part B: $[(P_U / P_N) -EPRA] * P_N =$
> $[(\$300 / \$580) - 0.0991] * \$580 = $ **$242.52**

> Therefore, our FPR is between $242.52 - $357.48.

In reference to my actual historical data selling this item, this is pretty accurate, and tells us that these are roughly the low and high points we should expect to sell at. True to form, I have always sought to buy this item for $250or less, and resell it for $350 or more.

Of course, this is not to say we would never see a sale below the lower boundary (like the times I purchased this item for $180and $230), or above the upper boundary (like the time I sold one for $360, plus I'm sure someone has sold a used one successfully for $400). However, it gives us a general idea of the estimated upper and lower bounds of the expected price fluctuations around the point P_U, our target midpoint during resale, without pushing our upper boundary too far beyond our defined point of Equilibrium.

Now let's look at how the Functional Price Range tightens up when there is less depreciation involved. The stereo compressor I referenced in Chapter 6 falls into this category. It was a Neve Portico 5043 Stereo Compressor, which tends to sell around $1,300 on the used market.

Neve Portico 5043 Stereo Compressor
Notice here that I have increased my profit threshold to $150, since this is a higher-dollar item.

1. $E = \$1,300$, $T = \$150$, $C = 0.25$, $P_N = \$1,800$
2. $P_U = [(2*\$1,300 - \$150) * 0.5] = \$1,225$
3. $D = [1 - (\$1,300 / \$1,800)] = 0.2777$
4. $EPRA = (0.2777) * (0.25) = 0.0694$, or **6.94%**
5. $FPR = [(P_U / P_N) +/- EPRA] * P_N =$

    Part A: $[(P_U / P_N) + EPRA] * P_N =$
        $[(\$1,225 / \$1,800) + 0.0694] * \$1,800 = $ **$1,349.92**

    Part B: $[(P_U / P_N) - EPRA] * P_N =$
        $[(\$1,225 / \$580) - 0.0694] * \$580 = $ **$1,100.08**

Therefore, our FPR is between $1,100.08 - $1,349.92.

In reality, I purchased my 5043 for $1,130 at auction on eBay and resold it on Craigslist for $1,320 for a total profit of $190. This is nothing to complain about, and you can see how this fits into the boundaries established by our Functional Price Range estimate above.

However, notably – the EPRA is smaller here (6.94%) compared to the previous example with the Epiphone Les Paul Standard (9.91%). Since the EPRA applies in both positive *and* negative directions in computing our FPR, we can double our EPRAs to compare the total differences in price swing:

$2 * EPRA =$ Total Price Swing

Epiphone Les Paul Standard – 2 * 9.91% = **19.82%**
Neve Portico 5043 Stereo Compressor – 2 * 6.94% = **13.88%**

The total difference, then, between the two scenarios is 5.94%. This might not seem like much, but considering this percentage is multiplied by the *new* price in determining our price range, it can be significant for these higher-priced items like my compressor. 0.0594 * \$1,800 = \$106.92, over a full hundred dollars of price swing "lost" due to the effects of a shrinking price range resulting from less depreciation.

In your day-to-day operations, performing this math is not actually necessary to "figure out" what to do in a given situation. I simply walk you through it here to describe the thought process I naturally go through when evaluating deals. When I have already estimated my Equilibrium Price, I can then compare it to the retail price of the item and run through this formula quickly in my head to approximate the potential upper and lower bounds of the price range I should be working in (in terms of my buy and sell prices).

Despite what the math may suggest, this is truly more an art than a science, but I lay out the formula here since this is in fact how I think through things when conducting data analysis. On a day-to-day basis, it is probably more helpful to simply realize that your opportunity decreases (along with your profit margin) on items with less depreciation, whereas items with more depreciation are often the best opportunities.

The only caveat to this is if you happen to get lucky and find an item that normally exhibits low depreciation selling for way under its Equilibrium Price. For instance, if you were to find a Neve Portico 5043 Stereo Compressor selling for \$750 from someone desperate for the cash, it would be an insane deal, since you know the market will easily allow you to resell upwards of \$1,200-1,300. These lucky situations will happen less often, but be more of a "sure thing" when they do arise.

APPENDIX E

RECOMMENDED READING

The following is a list of books on negotiation, sales, mental toughness, interpersonal communications, and general self-improvement. These books have helped me achieve higher levels of awareness and insight with regard to these topics, and I highly recommend them as additional learning resources.

- *The Way of the Seal* by Mark Divine
- *How to Pitch Anything* by Oren Klaff
- *The Way of the Shepherd* by Dr. Kevin Leman
- *Emotional Intelligence 2.0* by Travis Bradberry
- *48 Laws of Power* by Robert Greene
- *Negotiating Tactics: Bargain Your Way to Winning* by Edward Levin
- *Mastering Communication at Work* by Ethan Becker
- *The Art of War* by Sun Tzu
- *Tricks of the Mind* by Derren Brown
- *The Game* by Neil Strauss
- *The Art of Learning* by Josh Waitzkin

Some of these books, such as *How to Pitch Anything* and *Negotiating Tactics: Bargain Your Way to Winning* are fairly specifically about selling and/or negotiating. However, the other books offer additional insights into the human dynamics that play into every interaction you will ever have, whether business or personal.

In fact, if you are the type of person who struggles to manage your own emotions or understand the emotions of others, I would urge you to read *Emotional Intelligence 2.0*. This book offers practical insights that you can apply in a matter of minutes toward getting your emotional life under control. For me, personally, this book was immensely helpful in gaining control over my emotions. On top of that, it opened my eyes to new ways of looking at interpersonal situations that were very insightful.

Along the same lines, another book that was particularly motivating and inspired much change in my life was *The Way of the Seal*. It is written by Mark Divine, a former Navy Seal Commander, who has been quite successful in the military, in business, and in his personal life. The insights contained within are priceless, especially with regards to leadership and self-management.

ABOUT THE AUTHOR

Steven Fies is a business professional with a passion for playing guitar, surfing, and spending quality time with his family. In his first sales position, he took the desk of a former rep whose annual sales volume was $225,000 and increased it to $500,000 within fourteen months. He holds a bachelor's degree in Management Science from the University of California, San Diego, and currently lives in Austin, Texas with his wife and two dogs.

Made in United States
North Haven, CT
07 December 2021